Prayer for Each Day

Prayer
for Each Day

Taizé

GIA Publications, Inc.
Chicago

CASSELL
London

British Library Cataloguing-in-Publication Data
A catalogue record for this book is available from the British Library.

GIA ISBN: 1-57999-029-0
(USA, Canada, and USA dependencies)

Cassell ISBN: 0-304-70444-X
(Rest of the world)

Cassell
Wellington House, 125 Strand, London WC2R 0BB

GIA Publications, Inc.
7404 S. Mason Ave., Chicago, IL 60638

From the depths of the human condition a secret aspiration rises up. Caught in the anonymous rhythms of schedules and timetables, men and women of today are implicitly thirsting for an essential reality, for an inner life.

Nothing is more conducive to a communion with the living God than a meditative common prayer with, as its high point, singing that never ends and that continues in the silence of one's heart when one is alone again. When the mystery of God becomes tangible through the simple beauty of symbols, when it is not smothered by too many words, then prayer with others, far from exuding monotony and boredom, awakens us to heaven's joy on earth.

For many Christians down through the ages, a few words repeated endlessly have been a road to contemplation. When these words are sung, then perhaps they have even more of an impact on the whole personality, penetrating its very depths.

To celebrate such an all-inclusive prayer only a few people are needed, and already the heart becomes more encompassing in an encounter with Christ. And in addition, if these people were to join, at least once a week, the prayer of the local Christian community, the worship of a parish or congregation where all the generations are present, including little children, young adults and elderly persons, then the universality of communion in Christ would find a clear expression.

Prayer is a serene force at work within human beings, stirring them up, changing their hearts, never allowing them to close their eyes in the face of evil, of wars, of all that threatens the innocent of this world. From it we draw the energy to wage other struggles, to transform the human condition and to make the earth a place fit to live in.

All who walk in the footsteps of Christ, while holding themselves in the presence of God, remain alongside other people as well. They do not separate prayer and solidarity with others.

—BROTHER ROGER OF TAIZÉ

Table of Contents

Introduction

This book offers a collection of prayer formats adapted to the different seasons of the liturgical year in order to make it possible for one or many persons to pray regularly. The elements it contains can also be used separately or combined in different ways to prepare group prayers.

The liturgical year offers us a way of following the stages of Christ's life: the season of Advent leading up to Christmas, then the season of Lent culminating in Holy Week, and finally the season of Easter which lasts until Pentecost. The weeks between these seasons make up the time of the Church.

Fourteen prayers are proposed for the time of the Church, thus making a two-week cycle possible. For each of the seasons of Advent, Lent and Easter, a week-long cycle is offered. For Christmas, Holy Week and Pentecost, three prayers are provided.

The other feasts of the liturgical year are not mentioned in order not to overload the book. The fourteenth prayer of the time of the Church, however, is useful for celebrating the memory of holy women and men of the past: the apostles, Mary, the first person who said yes to Christ, the martyrs, and so on. In this way, our prayer sets us within the communion of all believers.

THE ORDER OF A PRAYER

To begin the prayer, choose one or two songs of praise.

PSALM

Jesus prayed these age-old prayers of his people. Christians have always found in them a wellspring of life. The psalms

1

place us in the great communion of all believers. Our joys and sorrows, our trust in God, our thirst and even our anguish find expression in the psalms.

One or two persons can alternate in reading or singing the verses of a psalm. After each verse, all respond with an Alleluia or another sung acclamation. If the verses are sung they should be short, usually two lines. In some cases, the congregation can hum the final chord of the acclamation while the solo verses are being sung. If the verses are read and not sung, they can be longer. A choice of accessible verses has been made for each prayer. If other psalms are used, do not hesitate to choose just a few verses, the most accessible ones. It is not necessary to read the entire psalm.

READING

Reading Scripture is a way of going to "the inexhaustible wellspring by which God gives himself to thirsting human beings" (Origen, third century). The Bible is a "letter from God to creatures" that enables them "to discover God's heart in God's words" (Gregory the Great, sixth century).

Communities who pray regularly customarily read the books of the Bible in systematic fashion. But for a weekly or monthly prayer, more accessible readings should be chosen, as well as ones which fit the theme of the prayer or the season. In this book we have chosen to offer some key texts that require no explanation. If a shorter reading is desired, only the part printed in bold characters can be read. To complete this choice of Biblical texts, the bimonthly Letter from Taizé proposes a short reading for every day of the year.

Each reading can be begun by saying "A reading from..." or "The Gospel according to Saint...." If there are two readings, the first can be chosen from the Old Testament, the Epistles, the Acts of the Apostles or the Book of Revelation; the second should always be from one of the Gospels. In that case, a meditative song can be sung between the readings.

Before or after the reading, it is a good idea to choose a song celebrating the light of Christ. While this is being sung, children or young people can come forward with candles to light an oil lamp set on a lampstand. This symbol reminds us that, even when the night is very dark, whether in our own life or in the life of humanity, Christ's love is a fire that never goes out.

SONG

SILENCE

When we try to express communion with God in words, our minds quickly come up short. But, in the depths of our being, through the Holy Spirit, Christ is praying far more than we imagine.

Although God never stops trying to communicate with us, God never wants to impose anything. Often God's voice is heard only in a whisper, in a breath of silence. Remaining in silence in God's presence, open to the Holy Spirit, is already prayer.

The road to contemplation is not one of achieving inner silence at all costs by following some technique that creates a kind of emptiness within. If, instead, with a childlike trust we let Christ pray silently within us, then one day we shall discover that the depths of our being are inhabited by a Presence.

During a time of prayer with others, it is best to have just one fairly long period of silence (5-10 minutes) rather than several shorter ones. If those taking part in the prayer are not used to silence, it can help to explain it briefly beforehand. Or, after the song immediately preceding the silence, someone can say, "The prayer will now continue with a few moments of silence."

INTERCESSIONS OR LITANY OF PRAISE

A prayer composed of short petitions or acclamations, sustained by humming, with each petition followed by a response sung by all, can form a kind of "pillar of fire" at the heart of the prayer. Praying for others widens our prayer to the dimensions of the entire human family; we entrust to God the joys and the hopes, the sorrows and the sufferings of all people, particularly those who are forgotten. A prayer of praise enables us to celebrate all that God is for us.

One or two persons can take turns expressing the petitions or the acclamations of praise, which are introduced and followed by a response such as *Kyrie eleison, Gospodi pomiluj* ("Lord, have mercy"), or *Praise to you, Lord.* After the written petitions or acclamations are finished, time may be left for people to pray spontaneously in their own words, expressing prayers that rise up from their hearts. These spontaneous prayers should be brief and be addressed to God; they should not become an excuse for communicating one's own ideas and opinions to other people by formulating them as a prayer. Each of these spontaneous prayers should be followed by the same response sung by all.

OUR FATHER

CONCLUDING PRAYER

The prayers suggested are chosen from among those written by Brother Roger.

SONGS

At the end, the singing can go on for some time. A small group can remain to sustain the singing of those who wish to keep on praying.

Other people can be invited for a time of small-group sharing nearby, for example by reflecting together on a Bible text, perhaps using the "Johannine hours." Each month in the *Letter from Taizé* "Johannine hours" are proposed, a time of silence and sharing around a text from Scripture.

PREPARING A WELCOMING SPACE
FOR A MEDITATIVE PRAYER

When possible, it is preferable to meet in a church, making it beautiful and welcoming. The way the space is arranged is important for the quality of the prayer. Naturally it is not necessary to do a complete restoration of the church; very simple means can be used to create a prayerful atmosphere. If it is not possible to meet in a church, it is important to make the prayer-space as harmonious as you can.

It is preferable for all the participants to face the same direction during the prayer, as a way of expressing that we pray not to one another but to Christ.

A place of prayer can be made welcoming with very little: a cross, an open Bible, some candles, icons, flowers. The lighting should be subdued, not glaring. Place a carpet in the center for those who wish to pray while kneeling or sitting on the ground; chairs or benches should also be available around the edges for those who prefer to sit on them.

It is helpful to welcome people as they enter, giving them the song-sheet and inviting them to come forward.

Leading the prayer is a service to others. It entails preparing the prayer and making sure it goes forward in a way that allows everyone to remain focused on the essential, with no distractions. Once the prayer has begun, there should be no technical announcements or explanations that interrupt the flow.

In the fourth century, Saint John Chrysostom wrote, "The home is a little church." Today, in secularized societies, by using some symbols of Christ, our dwellings can give glimpses of an invisible presence. A corner in every home, no matter how small, can be set aside for prayer, for example with an icon, a candle, a Bible.

ICONS

Icons contribute to the beauty of worship. They are like windows open on the realities of the Kingdom of God, making them present in our prayer on earth.

Although icons are images, they are not simply illustrations or decorations. They are symbols of the incarnation, a presence which offers to the eyes the spiritual message that the Word addresses to the ears.

According to the eighth-century theologian Saint John Damascene, icons are based on the coming of Christ to earth. Our salvation is linked to the incarnation of the divine Word, and therefore to matter: "In the past, the incorporeal and invisible God was never represented. But now that God has been manifested in the flesh and has dwelt among men, I represent the visible in God. I do not adore matter; I adore the creator of matter, who has become matter for my sake, who chose to dwell within matter and who, through matter, has caused my salvation" (*Discourse* I,16).

By the faith it expresses, by its beauty and its depth, an icon can create a space of peace and sustain an expectant waiting. It invites us to welcome salvation even in the flesh and in creation.

PRAYER AROUND THE CROSS
AND THE FESTIVAL OF THE RESURRECTION

From the beginning Christians have recalled each week the deepest mystery of their faith, the "passover" from death to life that Christ undertook and that he continues to undertake in the lives of human beings. Every week can thus conclude with the celebration of the dead and risen Christ.

Christ's passover from death to life can be celebrated on two successive evenings, Friday and Saturday, or else in a single service. At the end of one of the prayers in this book, the particular celebration can be added.

Prayer around the cross is a way of expressing an invisible communion not only with the crucified Jesus but with all who suffer–all the victims of abandonment, abuse, discrimination or torture, all those condemned to silence. In the center of the Church the icon of the cross is laid flat, resting on a couple of low stools or cushions and illuminated by a few candles. While the meditative singing continues, those who wish to do so come up to the cross to pray. They can make a gesture, such as placing their forehead on the wood of the cross, as a sign that they are entrusting silently to Christ all that burdens them as well as the difficulties of other people, both those they know personally and those who are far away: the oppressed, the ill, the poor, the persecuted. This prayer reminds us that here and now, risen from the dead, Christ accompanies every human being in his or her suffering, even when his presence is not recognized.

A festival of the light of Christ is a way of celebrating the resurrection which, for each person, already begins invisibly here on earth. Upon entering the church, which should be dimly lit, everyone receives a small candle. While a song of resurrection is sung, each person's candle is lit, until the whole church is full of light. This is a sign of the light of Christ, which also symbolizes our identity as Christians as children of the light. Then one of the Gospel accounts of the resurrection can be read, followed by more joyful meditative singing.

THE CROSS ON PILGRIMAGE

The icon of the cross itself can be brought from place to place, thus creating a bond of communion between groups, parishes and families. When a cross sets out on pilgrimage, a whole life of prayer springs up around it. Passing an icon from one community to another makes our fellowship concrete; it is like a sign of Christ who comes to visit every human being without exception. It is also a way of living out reconciliation, of creating ties between very different persons and groups.

This sign of reconciliation is very powerful when the places the cross goes to are as diverse as possible. It can be present for the usual prayer of a parish or congregation, of a family or group. It can be welcomed in places of suffering and exclusion by people who live in solidarity with those in need. A prayer around the cross can be made up simply of a short period of silence, a few songs, a Bible reading and some intercessions.

MEDITATIVE SINGING

Singing is one of the most essential elements of worship. Short chants, repeated again and again, give it a meditative character. Using just a few words they express a basic reality of faith, quickly grasped by the mind. As the words are sung over many times, this reality gradually penetrates the whole being. Meditative singing thus becomes a way of listening to God. It allows everyone to take part in a time of prayer together and to remain together in attentive waiting on God, without having to fix the length of time too exactly.

To open the gates of trust in God, nothing can replace the beauty of human voices united in song. This beauty can give us a glimpse of "heaven's joy on earth," as Eastern Christians put it. And an inner life begins to blossom within us.

These songs also sustain personal prayer. Through them, little by little, our being finds an inner unity in God. They can continue in the silence of our hearts when we are at work, speaking with others or resting. In this way prayer and daily life are united. They allow us to keep on praying even when we are unaware of it, in the silence of our hearts.

The "songs of Taizé" published in different languages are simple, but preparation is required to use them in prayer. This preparation should take place before the prayer itself, so that once it begins the atmosphere remains meditative.

During the prayer it is better if no one directs the music; in this way everyone can face the cross, the icons or the altar. (In a large congregation, however, it may be necessary for someone to direct, as discreetly as possible, a small group of instruments or singers who support the rest, always remembering that they are not giving a performance for the others.) The person who begins the songs is generally up front, together with those who will read the psalm, the reading and the intercessions, not facing the others but turned like them towards the altar or the icons. If a song is begun spontaneously, the pitch is generally too low. A tuning-fork or pitch-pipe can help, or a musical instrument give the first note or accompany the melody. Make sure the tempo does not slow down too much, as this tends to happen when the singing goes on for some time. As the number of participants increases, it becomes necessary to use a microphone, preferably hand-held, to begin and end the songs (they can be ended by singing "Amen" on the final note). The person who begins the singing can support the others by singing into a microphone, being careful not to drown out the other voices. A good sound-system is essential if the congregation is large; if necessary, check it before the prayer and try it out with those who will be using the microphones.

Songs in many different languages are appropriate for large international gatherings. In a neighborhood prayer with people of all ages present, most of the songs should be in languages actually understood by some of the participants, or in Latin. If possible, give each person a song sheet or booklet. You can also include one or two well-known local songs or hymns.

Instruments: a guitar or keyboard instrument can support the harmonic structure of the songs. They are especially helpful in keeping the correct pitch and tempo. Guitars should be played in classical, not folk style. A microphone may be necessary for them to be heard. In addition to this basic accompaniment, there are parts for other instruments.

For more details, including solo verses and instrumental parts, see the different editions of Music from Taizé.

PERSONAL PRAYER

A humble prayer is something accessible to everyone. Expressing our innermost longings to Christ in utter freedom and great simplicity, we can entrust all our burdens to him. God does not ask for marvels beyond our capacities nor superhuman efforts in our praying. Countless believers have had an intense prayer-life using a few simple words. The apostle Paul wrote that "we do not know how to pray as we ought...." And he added, "...but the Holy Spirit comes to help us in our weakness and prays within us" (Romans 8,26).

There are many ways we can express our personal prayer—gestures like the sign of the cross or like the disciples' posture at the end of Luke's Gospel, bowing low with their foreheads touching the ground. Praying in this way expresses our deep desire to renew the gift of our life at every moment.

Some people pray using many words, others just a few, always the same, in a short prayer that expresses an inner call. This kind of praying is not a "method." But in the course of our day, such a short prayer can bring us out of ourselves and lead us to the wellspring:

In all things peace of heart, joy, simplicity and mercy.

God buries our past in the heart of Christ and will take care of our future.

Christ Jesus, inner light, let me welcome your love; may I find joy.

I love you, perhaps not as I would like to, but I do love you.

Holy Spirit, Spirit of the risen Christ, you fill us with your constant presence; come and quench our thirst for trust, peace and forgiveness, to such an extent that the wellsprings of jubilation never run dry.

Advent

By preparing us for Christmas, Advent prepares us to welcome Christ.

In the life of the people of Israel, God prepared the coming of Christ. The prophets announced his coming; John the Baptist opened the way. Advent reminds us of the longing of God's poor: Mary and Joseph, Elizabeth and Zechariah....

Advent is also a time of longing for Christ's presence in us and, through us, in the world. This longing is made up of simplicity, the spirit of childhood and joy.

Advent 1

PSALM

O Lord, you once favored your land
and revived the fortunes of Jacob,
you forgave the guilt of your people
and covered all their sins.

Will you not restore again our life
that your people may rejoice in you?
Let us see, O Lord, your mercy
and give us your saving help.

I will hear what the Lord has to say
a voice that speaks of peace,
peace for his people and friends
and those who turn to God in their hearts.
Salvation is near for the God-fearing,
and Glory will dwell in our land.

Mercy and faithfulness have met;
justice and peace have embraced.
Faithfulness shall spring from the earth
and justice look down from heaven.

The Lord will make us prosper
and our earth shall yield its fruit.
Justice shall march in the forefront
and peace shall follow the way.

from Psalm 85

READING

Paul wrote: Rejoice in the Lord always; again I will say, Rejoice. Let your gentleness be known to everyone. The Lord is near. Do not worry about anything, but in everything by prayer and supplication with thanksgiving let your requests be made known to God. And the peace of God, which surpasses all understanding, will guard your hearts and your minds in Christ Jesus.

Philippians 4,4-7

or

The beginning of the good news of Jesus Christ, the Son of God. As it is written in the prophet Isaiah, "See, I am sending my messenger ahead of you, who will prepare your way; the voice of one crying out in the wilderness: Prepare the way of the Lord, make his paths straight," John the baptizer appeared in the wilderness, proclaiming a baptism of repentance for the forgiveness of sins. And people from the whole Judean countryside and all the people of Jerusalem were going out to him, and were baptized by him in the river Jordan, confessing their sins. Now **John was clothed with camel's hair, with a leather belt around his waist, and he ate locusts and wild honey. He proclaimed, "The one who is more powerful than I is coming after me; I am not worthy to stoop down and untie the thong of his sandals. I have baptized you with water; but he will baptize you with the Holy Spirit."**

Mark 1,1-8

SONG

SILENCE

16

INTERCESSIONS

O Wisdom, coming from the mouth of the Most High! You reign over all things from one end of the earth to the other; come and teach us the way of wisdom.
–Lord Jesus, come soon!

O Lord and Head of the house of Israel, you appeared to Moses in the fire of the burning bush and gave him the Law on Sinai; come with outstretched arm and ransom us.
–Lord Jesus, come soon!

O Morning Star, Splendor of Light eternal and bright Sun of justice; come and shine on all who live in darkness and in the shadow of death.
–Lord Jesus, come soon!

O King of the nations, you alone can fulfill their desires; Cornerstone, you make opposing nations one; come and save us. You formed us all from clay.
–Lord Jesus, come soon!

O Emmanuel, Hope of the nations and their Savior; come and save us, Lord our God.
–Lord Jesus, come soon!

The Spirit and the Bride say, Come!
–Amen! Lord Jesus, come soon!

OUR FATHER

PRAYER

Jesus, joy of our hearts, your Gospel assures us that the Kingdom of God is in our midst, and the gates of simplicity, and those of innocence, open within us.

or

Bless us, Christ Jesus; in you our heart finds joy.

SONGS

Advent 2

PSALM

To you, O Lord, I lift up my soul,
to you, my God.

My God, I trust you, let me not be disappointed;
do not let my enemies triumph.
Those who hope in you shall not be disappointed,
but only those who wantonly break faith.

Lord, make me know your ways.
Lord, teach me your paths.
Make me walk in your truth and teach me,
for you are God my savior.

In you I hope all the day long
because of your goodness, O Lord.
Remember your mercy, Lord,
and the love you have shown from of old.
Do not remember the sins of years past.
In your love remember me.

The Lord is good and upright,
showing the path to those who stray,
guiding the humble in the right path,
and teaching the way to the poor.

from Psalm 25

READING

Paul wrote: Rejoice always, pray without ceasing, give thanks in all circumstances; for this is the will of God in Christ Jesus for you. Do not quench the Spirit. Do not despise the words of prophets, but test everything; hold fast to what is good; abstain from every form of evil. **May the God of peace himself sanctify you entirely; and may your spirit and soul and body be kept sound and blameless at the coming of our Lord Jesus Christ. The one who calls you is faithful, and he will do this.**

1 Thessalonians 5,16-24

or

Jesus said to Nicodemus, "Very truly, I tell you, no one can see the kingdom of God without being born from above." Nicodemus said to him, "How can anyone be born after having grown old? Can one enter a second time into the mother's womb and be born?" Jesus answered, "Very truly, I tell you, no one can enter the kingdom of God without being born of water and Spirit. What is born of the flesh is flesh, and what is born of the Spirit is spirit. Do not be astonished that I said to you, You must be born from above. The wind blows where it chooses, and you hear the sound of it, but you do not know where it comes from or where it goes. So it is with everyone who is born of the Spirit."

John 3,3-8

SONG

SILENCE

INTERCESSIONS

God our Father, we bless you for having called us to know you, to love you and to live with you.
–Maranatha, the Lord is coming!

You sent your beloved Son, your perfect image and the reflection of your face; he became like us in all things but sin.
–Maranatha, the Lord is coming!

In him you proclaimed the good news of your Kingdom; you forgive our offenses and heal our wounds.
–Maranatha, the Lord is coming!

Keep us in the communion of your Son; keep us alert as we wait for the day of his coming.
–Maranatha, the Lord is coming!

Give us your peace, so that we can communicate it to one another in mutual love, and serve the human family.
–Maranatha, the Lord is coming!

OUR FATHER

PRAYER

Jesus our joy, the simple desire for your presence is already the beginning of faith. And, in our life, the hidden event of a longing causes wellsprings to gush forth: kindness, generosity, and also that inner harmony which comes from the Holy Spirit in us.

or

Bless us, Lord Christ; you give us a Gospel freshness when a heart that trusts is at the beginning of everything

SONGS

Advent 3

PSALM

The heavens proclaim the glory of God,
and the firmament shows forth the work of God's hands.
Day unto day takes up the story
and night unto night makes known the message.

No speech, no word, no voice is heard
yet their span extends through all the earth,
their words to the utmost bounds of the world.

There God has placed a tent for the sun;
it comes forth like a bridegroom coming from his tent,
rejoices like a champion to run its course.

At the end of the sky is the rising of the sun;
to the furthest end of the sky is its course.
There is nothing concealed from its burning heat.

from Psalm 19

READING

I will greatly rejoice in the Lord, my whole being shall exult in
my God; for he has clothed me with the garments of salvation,
he has covered me with the robe of righteousness, as a bridegroom decks himself with a garland, and as a bride adorns her-
self with her jewels. For as the earth brings forth its shoots, and
as a garden causes what is sown in it to spring up, so the Lord
God will cause righteousness and praise to spring up before all

the nations.

Isaiah 61,10-11

or

In the sixth month the angel Gabriel was sent by God to a town in Galilee called Nazareth, to a virgin engaged to a man whose name was Joseph, of the house of David. The virgin's name was Mary. And he came to her and said, "Greetings, favored one! The Lord is with you." But she was much perplexed by his words and pondered what sort of greeting this might be. The angel said to her, "Do not be afraid, Mary, for you have found favor with God. And now, you will conceive in your womb and bear a son, and you will name him Jesus. He will be great, and will be called the Son of the Most High, and the Lord God will give to him the throne of his ancestor David. He will reign over the house of Jacob forever, and of his kingdom there will be no end." Mary said to the angel, "How can this be, since I am a virgin?" The angel said to her, "The Holy Spirit will come upon you, and the power of the Most High will overshadow you; therefore the child to be born will be holy; he will be called Son of God. And now, your relative Elizabeth in her old age has also conceived a son; and this is the sixth month for her who was said to be barren. For nothing will be impossible with God." Then Mary said, "Here am I, the servant of the Lord; let it be with me according to your word." Then the angel departed from her.

Luke 1,26-38

SONG

SILENCE

We give you thanks, O God, for revealing your love in
creation,
–We bless your holy name.

For human beings made in your image and called to live in your
communion,
–We bless your holy name.

For the promise of your reign in justice and peace, in holiness
and charity,
–We bless your holy name.

For the revelation of your Kingdom in our midst through your
Son, Jesus Christ,
–We bless your holy name.

For his humble birth and his holy life, for his words and his
miracles,
–We bless your holy name.

For his sufferings and his death, for his resurrection and his
entry into glory,
–We bless your holy name.

For your Church, called to be a place of communion for every
human being,
–We bless your holy name.

For the coming of your Kingdom within us by the gift of the
Holy Spirit,
–We bless your holy name.

By the coming of your Kingdom at the end of time, when you will be all in all,
–We bless your holy name.

OUR FATHER

PRAYER

God of all eternity, you know that our human language is almost incapable of expressing our longing for a communion with you. But you grant us the gift of a life hidden in you. And the sun rises on a new day, a day of trusting.

or

Christ Jesus, be our peace; you tell us: Don't be afraid; I am here.

SONGS

Advent 4

SONG

PSALM

Defend me, O God, and plead my cause
against a godless nation.
From a deceitful and cunning people
rescue me, O God.

Send forth your light and your truth;
let these be my guide.
Let them bring me to your holy mountain,
to the place where you dwell.

And I will come to your altar, O God,
the God of my joy.
My redeemer, I will thank you on the harp,
O God, my God.

Why are you cast down, my soul,
why groan within me?
Hope in God; I will praise yet again,
my savior and my God.

from Psalm 43

READING

A shoot shall come out from the stump of Jesse, and a branch
shall grow out of his roots. The spirit of the Lord shall rest
on him, the spirit of wisdom and understanding, the spirit of
counsel and might, the spirit of knowledge and the fear of the

Lord. His delight shall be in the fear of the Lord. He shall not judge by what his eyes see, or decide by what his ears hear; but with righteousness he shall judge the poor, and decide with equity for the meek of the earth. (...) Righteousness shall be the belt around his waist, and faithfulness the belt around his loins. The wolf shall live with the lamb, the leopard shall lie down with the kid, the calf and the lion and the fatling together, and a little child shall lead them. The cow and the bear shall graze, their young shall lie down together; and the lion shall eat straw like the ox. The nursing child shall play over the hole of the asp, and the weaned child shall put its hand on the adder's den. They will not hurt or destroy on all my holy mountain; for the earth will be full of the knowledge of the Lord as the waters cover the sea.

Isaiah 11,1-9

or

In those days Mary set out and went with haste to a Judean town in the hill country, where she entered the house of Zechariah and greeted Elizabeth. When Elizabeth heard Mary's greeting, the child leaped in her womb. And Elizabeth was filled with the Holy Spirit and exclaimed with a loud cry, "Blessed are you among women, and blessed is the fruit of your womb. And why has this happened to me, that the mother of my Lord comes to me? For as soon as I heard the sound of your greeting, the child in my womb leaped for joy. And blessed is she who believed that there would be a fulfillment of what was spoken to her by the Lord."

Luke 1,39-45

SONG

SILENCE

Renew in us, Lord, the joy of your call.
–Be with us, Lord Emmanuel!

Send upon us your Spirit of love: may we never shut our hearts to our neighbor.
–Be with us, Lord Emmanuel!

Renew the unity between Christians: may they manifest your love by their communion.
–Be with us, Lord Emmanuel!

Support those who suffer in their hearts or in their flesh: restore them to peace and health.
–Be with us, Lord Emmanuel!

Welcome those who have died into the life of eternity: may their eyes see the light that never sets.
–Be with us, Lord Emmanuel!

OUR FATHER

PRAYER

Jesus, light of our hearts, we would like to remain close to you, never abandoning you by our wayside. And when we come to know our weaknesses, unexpected resources appear within us. How could we refuse an inner vitality that comes from you?

or

May the peace of God, which is beyond all understanding, keep our hearts and our minds in Christ Jesus.

SONGS

Advent 5

SONG

PSALM

Out of the depths I cry to you, O Lord,
Lord, hear my voice!
O let your ears be attentive
to the voice of my pleading.

If you, O Lord, should mark our guilt,
Lord, who would survive?
But with you is found forgiveness:
for this we revere you.

My soul is waiting for the Lord.
I count on God's word.
My soul is longing for the Lord
more than those who watch for daybreak.

Because with the Lord there is mercy
and fullness of redemption.
Israel indeed God will redeem
from all its iniquity.

Psalm 130

READING

Comfort, O comfort my people, says your God. Speak tenderly to Jerusalem, and cry to her that she has served her term, that her penalty is paid, that she has received from the Lord's hand double for all her sins. A voice cries out: "In the wilderness prepare the way of the Lord, make straight in the desert a highway for our God. Every valley shall be lifted up, and every mountain and hill be made low; the uneven ground shall become level, and the rough places a plain. Then the glory of the Lord shall be revealed, and all people shall see it together, for the mouth of the Lord has spoken."

Isaiah 40,1-5

or

Mary said, "My soul magnifies the Lord, and my spirit rejoices in God my Savior, for he has looked with favor on the lowliness of his servant. Surely, from now on all generations will call me blessed; for the Mighty One has done great things for me, and holy is his name. His mercy is for those who fear him from generation to generation. He has shown strength with his arm; he has scattered the proud in the thoughts of their hearts. He has brought down the powerful from their thrones, and lifted up the lowly; he has filled the hungry with good things, and sent the rich away empty. He has helped his servant Israel, in remembrance of his mercy, according to the promise he made to our ancestors, to Abraham and to his descendants forever."

Luke 1,46-55

SONG

SILENCE

LITANY OF PRAISE

God our Father, you sent your only Son in order to reconcile all things in him.
–See, God is coming to my aid.

Son of the living God, you shared our humanity and you gave your life for the salvation of the world.
–See, God is coming to my aid.

Holy Spirit, you came down upon Christ and you pour out the Father's love upon all human beings.
–See, God is coming to my aid.

O Christ, may your incarnation and your birth make us love our human condition.
–See, God is coming to my aid.

May your faithfulness on earth make each of us faithful in our commitment.
–See, God is coming to my aid.

OUR FATHER

PRAYER

Christ Jesus, you were a human being; you know how humans aspire to inner peace. Our soul asks you: give us peace within. And in our darkness, you kindle the fire of your forgiveness and your compassion, a fire which never dies away.

or

Jesus our peace, where the trusting of faith has been shaken you make us bearers of your Gospel, and you keep us close to those who are paralyzed by doubt.

SONGS

Advent 6

PSALM

In you, O Lord, I take refuge.
Let me never be put to shame.
In your justice, set me free,
hear me and speedily rescue me.

Be a rock of refuge for me,
a mighty stronghold to save me,
for you are my rock, my stronghold.
For your name's sake, lead me and guide me.

Release me from the snares they have hidden
for you are my refuge, Lord.
Into your hands I commend my spirit.
It is you who will redeem me, Lord.

You who have seen my affliction
and taken heed of my soul's distress,
have not handed me over to the enemy,
but set my feet at large.

As for me, I trust in you, Lord;
I say: You are my God.
My life is in your hands, deliver me
from the hands of those who hate me.

Let your face shine on your servant.
Save me in your love.

from Psalm 31

READING

Sing aloud, O daughter Zion; shout, O Israel! Rejoice and exult with all your heart, O daughter Jerusalem! (...) You shall fear disaster no more. On that day it shall be said to Jerusalem: Do not fear, O Zion; do not let your hands grow weak. **The Lord, your God, is in your midst, a warrior who gives victory; he will rejoice over you with gladness, he will renew you in his love; he will exult over you with loud singing as on a day of festival.**

Zephaniah 3,14-18a

or

There was a man sent from God, whose name was John. He came as a witness to testify to the light, so that all might believe through him. He himself was not the light, but he came to testify to the light. The true light, which enlightens everyone, was coming into the world. He was in the world, and the world came into being through him; yet the world did not know him. He came to what was his own, and his own people did not accept him. But to all who received him, who believed in his name, he gave power to become children of God.

John 1,6-12

SONG

SILENCE

LITANY OF PRAISE

Jesus, you come to announce Good News to the poor:
–We bless your holy name.

Jesus, you come to reveal to us the joy of forgiveness:
–We bless your holy name.

Jesus, you show your love to those who felt excluded:
–We bless your holy name.

Jesus, you want your Gospel to be proclaimed in every place:
–We bless your holy name.

Jesus, you keep alive the hope of your Church:
–We bless your holy name.

Jesus, you come to dwell in our midst:
–We bless your holy name.

OUR FATHER

PRAYER

Savior of every life, may those who seek you rejoice. You tell us:
I am familiar with your trials and your poverty, and yet you are
filled. Filled with what? With the living springs, hidden in your
depths.

or

Bless us, living God; in baptism you clothed us with a new garment, which is Christ himself.

SONGS

Advent 7

O Lord, hear my voice when I call;
have mercy and answer.
Of you my heart has spoken:
Seek God's face.

Instruct me, Lord, in your way
on an even path lead me.
False witnesses rise against me,
breathing out fury.

I am sure I shall see the Lord's goodness
in the land of the living.
In the Lord, hold firm and take heart.
Hope in the Lord!

from Psalm 27

READING

Be patient, until the coming of the Lord. The farmer waits for
the precious crop from the earth, being patient with it until it
receives the early and the late rains. You also must be patient.
Strengthen your hearts, for the coming of the Lord is near.

James 5,7-8

or

Now the birth of Jesus the Messiah took place in this way.

When his mother Mary had been engaged to Joseph, but before they lived together, she was found to be with child from the Holy Spirit. Her husband Joseph, being a righteous man and unwilling to expose her to public disgrace, planned to dismiss her quietly. But just when he had resolved to do this, an angel of the Lord appeared to him in a dream and said, "Joseph, son of David, do not be afraid to take Mary as your wife, for the child conceived in her is from the Holy Spirit. She will bear a son, and you are to name him Jesus, for he will save his people from their sins." All this took place to fulfill what had been spoken by the Lord through the prophet: "Look, the virgin shall conceive and bear a son, and they shall name him Emmanuel," which means, "God is with us." When Joseph awoke from sleep, he did as the angel of the Lord commanded him; he took her as his wife.

Matthew 1,18-24

SONG

SILENCE

LITANY OF PRAISE

Christ Jesus, sent into the world so that we may live through you:
–Lord, come soon!

Christ Jesus, you remain alongside all whose life is held in contempt:
–Lord, come soon!

Christ Jesus, you establish a new covenant with us that will never be broken:
–Lord, come soon!

Christ Jesus, you enlighten the eyes of all who are in darkness:
–Lord, come soon!

Christ Jesus, you make our deserts blossom; you lead us towards the land of gladness:
–Lord, come soon!

Christ Jesus, Good News will be proclaimed to the poor and freedom to prisoners:
–Lord, come soon!

Christ Jesus, broken hearts will be healed, the starving filled:
–Lord, come soon!

Christ Jesus, the paths will be levelled and your glory will dwell in our land:
–Lord, come soon!

OUR FATHER

PRAYER

Jesus, love of all loving, in the ploughed-up earth of our lives you come to plant the trusting of faith. A small seed at first, faith can become within us one of the most unmistakable Gospel realities. It keeps alive the inexhaustible goodness of a human heart.

or

Bless us, Christ Jesus; in you our hearts find peace.

SONGS

Christmas

The Christmas season celebrates the birth and the manifestation of Christ, Sun of justice who comes to shine in our darkness.

On Christmas Day we celebrate the lowliness of God's presence among us. On Epiphany we celebrate the manifestation of that presence to the whole world, symbolized by the Wise Men. On the eve of his mission, the baptism of Jesus is his manifestation as God's beloved Son on whom the Holy Spirit rests.

Christmas   1

PSALM

Sing a new song to the Lord
who has worked wonders;
whose right hand and holy arm
have brought salvation.

The Lord has made known salvation;
has shown justice to the nations;
has remembered truth and love
for the house of Israel.

All the ends of the earth have seen
the salvation of our God.
Shout to the Lord, all the earth,
ring out your joy.

Sing psalms to the Lord with the harp,
with the sound of music.
With trumpets and the sound of the horn
acclaim the King, the Lord.

from Psalm 98

READING

Long ago God spoke to our ancestors in many and various
ways by the prophets, but in these last days he has spoken to
us by a Son, whom he appointed heir of all things, through
whom he also created the worlds. He is the reflection of God's

glory and the exact imprint of God's very being, and he sustains all things by his powerful word. When he had made purification for sins, he sat down at the right hand of the Majesty on high.

Hebrews 1,1-3

or

In those days a decree went out from Emperor Augustus that all the world should be registered. This was the first registration and was taken while Quirinius was governor of Syria. All went to their own towns to be registered. Joseph also went from the town of Nazareth in Galilee to Judea, to the city of David called Bethlehem, because he was descended from the house and family of David. He went to be registered with Mary, to whom he was engaged and who was expecting a child. While they were there, the time came for her to deliver her child. And she gave birth to her firstborn son and wrapped him in bands of cloth, and laid him in a manger, because there was no place for them in the inn. In that region there were shepherds living in the fields, keeping watch over their flock by night. Then an angel of the Lord stood before them, and the glory of the Lord shone around them, and they were terrified. But the angel said to them, "Do not be afraid; for see—I am bringing you good news of great joy for all the people: to you is born this day in the city of David a Savior, who is the Messiah, the Lord. This will be a sign for you: you will find a child wrapped in bands of cloth and lying in a manger." And suddenly there was with the angel a multitude of the heavenly host, praising God and saying, "Glory to God in the highest heaven, and on earth peace among those whom he favors!"

Luke 2,1-14

SONG

SILENCE

LITANY OF PRAISE

O Christ, the prophets foretold your coming, the poor longed to see you.
–Our heart finds joy in God.

The heavens celebrated your birth; the apostles, the martyrs and the faithful down through the ages repeated the song of the angels.
–Our heart finds joy in God.

Your Church praises you in every human language, for she has seen your salvation.
–Our heart finds joy in God.

Son of God, you humbled yourself and became a servant, raising us up to share in your glory.
–Our heart finds joy in God.

We were in darkness and you have given us light and strength, peace and joy.
–Our heart finds joy in God.

Lead us according to your loving will; make us a people who follow you in holiness.
–Our heart finds joy in God.

Give us generous hearts to hear your Word and produce in us abundant fruit.
–Our heart finds joy in God.

OUR FATHER

PRAYER

Jesus, son of the Virgin Mary, at Christmas you offer us the joyful message of your Gospel. All who listen, all who welcome the gifts of the Holy Spirit, by day as well as in the vigils of the night, discover that with very little faith, with almost nothing, they have everything.

or

Christ Jesus, humble shepherds found you in a stable. Come to us, so that we may advance towards the brightness of your presence, hidden within us. And our hearts can say to you: Jesus, my joy, my hope, my life.

SONGS

Christmas 2

I thank you, Lord, with all my heart,
you have heard the words of my mouth.
In the presence of the angels I will bless you.
I will adore before your holy temple.

I thank you for your faithfulness and love
which excel all we ever knew of you.
On the day I called, you answered;
you increased the strength of my soul.

All the rulers on earth shall thank you
when they hear the words of your mouth.
They shall sing of the Lord's ways:
"How great is the glory of the Lord."

The Lord is high yet looks on the lowly
and the haughty God knows from afar.
Though I walk in the midst of affliction
you give me life and frustrate my foes.

You stretch out your hand and save me,
your hand will do all things for me
Your love, O Lord, is eternal,
discard not the work of your hands.

Psalm 138

READING

We declare to you what was from the beginning, what we have heard, what we have seen with our eyes, what we have looked at and touched with our hands, concerning the word of life–this life was revealed, and we have seen it and testify to it, and declare to you the eternal life that was with the Father and was revealed to us–we declare to you what we have seen and heard so that you also may have fellowship with us; and truly our fellowship is with the Father and with his Son Jesus Christ. We are writing these things so that our joy may be complete.

1 John 1,1-4

or

And the Word became flesh and lived among us, and we have seen his glory, the glory as of a father's only son, full of grace and truth. (John testified to him and cried out, "This was he of whom I said, 'He who comes after me ranks ahead of me because he was before me.'") From his fullness we have all received, grace upon grace. The law indeed was given through Moses; grace and truth came through Jesus Christ. No one has ever seen God. It is God the only Son, who is close to the Father's heart, who has made him known.

John 1,14-18

SONG

SILENCE

LITANY OF PRAISE

Jesus, Son of the living God, splendor of the Father, eternal light.
–Lord, we praise you!

Jesus, King of glory, Sun of justice, son of the Virgin Mary.
–Lord, we praise you!

Jesus, Wonderful Counselor, Everlasting Lord, Prince of Peace.
–Lord, we praise you!

Jesus, gentle and humble of heart, our help and our refuge.
–Lord, we praise you!

Jesus, God of peace, friend of all, source of life and of holiness.
–Lord, we praise you!

Jesus, brother of the poor, goodness without measure, inexhaustible wisdom.
–Lord, we praise you!

Jesus, good shepherd, true light, our way and our life.
–Lord, we praise you!

OUR FATHER

PRAYER

Christ Jesus, from the beginning you were in God. When you
came to live among human beings, you made the humble trusting of faith accessible. And the day is coming when we can say:
I belong to Christ, I am Christ's.

or

Bless us, Christ Jesus; enable us to welcome your love.

or

Christ Jesus, inner light, in this Christmas season you send your peace upon us; it is kindness; it leads to a change in our lives. And then an inner voice arises in us, and that voice is already our prayer. If our lips keep silent, our heart speaks to you and listens to you. In this way, the will of your love is accomplished within us.

SONGS

Christmas 3

PSALM

O God, be gracious and bless us
and let your face shed its light upon us.
So will your ways be known upon earth
and all nations learn your saving help.

Let the peoples praise you, O God;
let all the peoples praise you.

Let the nations be glad and exult
for you rule the world with justice.
With fairness you rule the peoples,
you guide the nations on earth.

Let the peoples praise you, O God;
let all the peoples praise you.

The earth has yielded its fruit
for God, our God, has blessed us.
May God still give us blessing
till the ends of the earth stand in awe.

Let the peoples praise you, O God;
let all the peoples praise you.

Psalm 67

You shall know that I, the Lord, am your Savior and your Redeemer, the Mighty One of Jacob. Violence shall no more be heard in your land, devastation or destruction within your borders; you shall call your walls Salvation, and your gates Praise. The sun shall no longer be your light by day, nor for brightness shall the moon give light to you by night; but the Lord will be your everlasting light, and your God will be your glory. Your sun shall no more go down, or your moon withdraw itself; for the Lord will be your everlasting light, and your days of mourning shall be ended.

Isaiah 60,16b.18-20

or

In the time of King Herod, after Jesus was born in Bethlehem of Judea, wise men from the East came to Jerusalem, asking, "Where is the child who has been born king of the Jews? For we observed his star at its rising, and have come to pay him homage." When King Herod heard this, he was frightened, and all Jerusalem with him; and calling together all the chief priests and scribes of the people, he inquired of them where the Messiah was to be born. They told him, "In Bethlehem of Judea; for so it has been written by the prophet: 'And you, Bethlehem, in the land of Judah, are by no means least among the rulers of Judah; for from you shall come a ruler who is to shepherd my people Israel.'" Then Herod secretly called for the wise men and learned from them the exact time when the star had appeared. Then he sent them to Bethlehem, saying, "Go and search diligently for the child; and when you have found him, bring me word so that I may also go and pay him homage." When they had heard the king, they set out; and there, ahead of them, went the star that they had seen at its rising, until it stopped over the place where the child was. When they saw that the star had stopped, they were overwhelmed with joy. **On entering the house, the wise men saw the child with Mary his mother; and they knelt down and paid him homage. Then, opening their treasure chests, they offered him gifts of gold, frankincense, and myrrh.** And having been warned in a dream not to return to Herod, they left for their own country by another road.

Matthew 2,1-12

SONG

SILENCE

INTERCESSIONS

O Christ, Son of God, you were before the world began, and you came to earth to save us all: make us witnesses of this Good News.
–Lord, we bless your Name.

Sun of justice, you shone at the Father's side and illuminated the universe: give light to all who dwell in the shadow of death.
–Lord, we bless your Name.

You became a little child and were laid in a manger: renew in us the simplicity of childhood.
–Lord, we bless your Name.

King of glory, you accepted such an inconceivable humbling: give us hearts which are poor.
–Lord, we bless your Name.

You became our living bread and gave us eternal life: gladden our hearts by your Eucharist.
–Lord, we bless your Name.

OUR FATHER

PRAYER

Lord Christ, son of the Virgin Mary, we call you by name. And we tell you: receive our child's prayer, we want to entrust everything to you and to rejoice in what you accomplish in each one of us.

or

Bless us, Christ Jesus; your love comes to heal the wounds of our heart.

SONGS

Lent and Holy Week

Lent is a time of retreat before the Easter celebrations. It prepares us for the festival of our liberation. In communion with Christ in the desert, each Christian is invited during these forty days to a conversion, in other words to turn his or her entire being towards God. The joy of God's forgiveness sustains us on this journey. The alleluia, an expression of Easter joy, is replaced by another short acclamation, for example Misericordias Domini in aeternum cantabo *(I will sing for ever the mercies of the Lord).*

During Holy Week we follow Christ along the way of the cross, but already the joy of Easter illuminates this road with its light. Christians are united to the crucified Jesus and speak the words of his anguish. They include in these prayers of Christ all the suffering of every person who is going through trials.

Lent 1

SONG

PSALM

Happy those whose offense is forgiven,
whose sin is remitted.
O happy those to whom the Lord
imputes no guilt,
in whose spirit is no guile.

Now I have acknowledged my sins;
my guilt I did not hide
I said: "I will confess
my offense to the Lord."
And you, Lord, have forgiven
the guilt of my sin.

So let faithful people pray to you
in the time of need.
The floods of water may reach high
but they shall stand secure.
You are my hiding place, O Lord;
you save me from distress.

Rejoice, rejoice in the Lord,
exult, you just!
O come, ring out your joy,
all you upright of heart.

from Psalm 32

Thus says the Lord: Is not this the fast that I choose: to loose the bonds of injustice, to undo the thongs of the yoke, to let the oppressed go free, and to break every yoke? Is it not to share your bread with the hungry, and bring the homeless poor into your house; when you see the naked, to cover them, and not to hide yourself from your own kin? Then your light shall break forth like the dawn, and your healing shall spring up quickly; your vindicator shall go before you, the glory of the Lord shall be your rear guard.

Isaiah 58,6-8

or

Jesus said: Whenever you pray, go into your room and shut the door and pray to your Father who is in secret; and your Father who sees in secret will reward you. (...) And whenever you fast, do not look dismal, like the hypocrites, for they disfigure their faces so as to show others that they are fasting. Truly I tell you, they have received their reward. But when you fast, put oil on your head and wash your face, so that your fasting may be seen not by others but by your Father who is in secret; and your Father who sees in secret will reward you.

Matthew 6,6.16-18

SONG

SILENCE

INTERCESSIONS

God our Father, you want us to become new creatures in Christ. We pray to you.

Lord, you promise us new heavens and a new earth. Renew our hope.

You have freed us from our slavery by giving us your only Son; you open for us the way of freedom.

Enable us to listen to your Word and to welcome it with hearts filled with love.

We were dead and you brought us to life through the Spirit; we were sinners and you continually restore us to purity of heart.

OUR FATHER

PRAYER

With you, Risen Christ, we go forward from one discovery to another. As we try to find out what you want from us, our life opens up to the Holy Spirit. And the Spirit comes to bring to fulfillment in us things we did not even dare hope for.

or

God of peace, you do not want us to know relentless worry but rather a humble repentance of heart. It is like a surge of trusting that enables us to place our faults in you. And then, by the inner light of forgiveness, little by little we discover a peace of heart.

or

Living God, you bury our past in the heart of Christ and are going to take care of our future.

SONGS

Lent 2

PSALM

My God, I trust you, let me not be disappointed;
do not let my enemies triumph.
Those who hope in you shall not be disappointed,
but only those who wantonly break faith.

Lord, make me know your ways.
Lord, teach me your paths.
Make me walk in your truth, and teach me,
for you are God my savior.

In you I hope all the day long
because of your goodness, O Lord.
Remember your mercy, Lord,
and the love you have shown from of old.
Do not remember the sins of my youth.
In your love remember me.

The Lord is good and upright,
showing the path to those who stray,
guiding the humble in the right path,
and teaching the way to the poor.

from Psalm 25

READING

Paul wrote: God, who is rich in mercy, out of the great love
with which he loved us even when we were dead through our

58

trespasses, made us alive together with Christ—by grace you have been saved—and raised us up with him and seated us with him in the heavenly places in Christ Jesus.

Ephesians 2,4-6

or

Jesus said to his disciples, "The Son of Man must undergo great suffering, and be rejected by the elders, chief priests, and scribes, and be killed, and on the third day be raised." Then he said to them all, **"If any want to become my followers, let them deny themselves and take up their cross daily and follow me.** For those who want to save their life will lose it, and those who lose their life for my sake will save it. What does it profit them if they gain the whole world, but lose or forfeit themselves?"

Luke 9,22-25

SONG

SILENCE

INTERCESSIONS

For the victims of war and violence, O God, we pray.

For those wounded by the constraints and the harshness of life, O God, we pray.

For the elderly and the ill who are alone, O God, we pray.

For those who devote their energies to restoring peace, to creating justice, to helping those who suffer, O God, we pray.

O Christ, you died and rose for us so that nothing can ever separate us from the love of God.

OUR FATHER

PRAYER

Christ of compassion, through your Gospel we discover that measuring what we are or what we are not leads nowhere. What matters is the humble trusting of faith. By it we are led to glimpse the innocence of God and to understand that "all God can do is give his love."

or

Bless us, Christ Jesus; you come to clothe us in compassion as in a garment.

SONGS

Lent 3

Have mercy on me, God, in your kindness.
In your compassion blot out my offense.
O wash me more and more from my guilt
and cleanse me from my sin.

My offenses truly I know them;
my sin is always before me.
Against you, you alone, have I sinned;
what is evil in your sight I have done.

Indeed you love truth in the heart;
then in the secret of my heart teach me wisdom.
O purify me, then I shall be clean;
O wash me, I shall be whiter than snow.

A pure heart create for me, O God,
put a steadfast spirit within me.
Do not cast me away from your presence,
nor deprive me of your holy spirit.

from Psalm 51

The hand of the Lord came upon me, and he brought me out
by the spirit of the Lord and set me down in the middle of a valley; it was full of bones. He led me all around them; there were
very many lying in the valley, and they were very dry. (...) Then

the Lord said to me, "Prophesy to the breath, prophesy, mortal, and say to the breath: Thus says the Lord God: Come from the four winds, O breath, and breathe upon these slain, that they may live." I prophesied as he commanded me, and the breath came into them, and they lived, and stood on their feet, a vast multitude. Then he said to me, "Mortal, these bones are the whole house of Israel. They say: Our bones are dried up, and our hope is lost; we are cut off completely. Therefore prophesy, and say to them: **Thus says the Lord God: I am going to open your graves, and bring you up from your graves, O my people; and I will bring you back to the land of Israel. And you shall know that I am the Lord, when I open your graves, and bring you up from your graves, O my people. I will put my spirit within you, and you shall live, and I will place you on your own soil; then you shall know that I, the Lord, have spoken and will act,"** says the Lord.

Ezekiel 37,1-2.9-14

or

Jesus said, "**I am the bread of life. Whoever comes to me will never be hungry, and whoever believes in me will never be thirsty.** (...)Everything that the Father gives me will come to me, and anyone who comes to me I will never drive away; for I have come down from heaven, not to do my own will, but the will of him who sent me. And this is the will of him who sent me, that I should lose nothing of all that he has given me, but raise it up on the last day. This is indeed the will of my Father, that all who see the Son and believe in him may have eternal life; and I will raise them up on the last day."

John 6.35-40

SONG

SILENCE

INTERCESSIONS

O Christ, you offer us healing; may we live by your life.

O Christ, you renew our hope; may we live by your life.

O Christ, you sat at table with sinners; may we live by your life.

O Christ, you raised up your friend Lazarus; may we live by your life.

O Christ, you forgave Peter when he repudiated you and you called him to follow you; may we live by your life.

O Christ, in you our resurrection has already begun; may we live by your life.

OUR FATHER

PRAYER

God of every human being, keep us from digging "cracked cisterns that do not hold the living water." We want to entrust ourselves to you, surrendering to you our worries and our entire lives.

or

Bless us, Christ Jesus; you love us always, even in our night.

SONGS

Lent 4

PSALM

Turn your ear, O Lord, and give answer
for I am poor and needy.
Preserve my life, for I am faithful;
save the servant who trusts in you.

You are my God, have mercy on me, Lord,
for I cry to you all the day long.
Give joy to your servant, O Lord,
for to you I lift up my soul.

O Lord, you are good and forgiving,
full of love to all who call.
Give heed, O Lord, to my prayer
and attend to the sound of my voice.

In the day of distress I will call
and surely you will reply.
Among the gods there is none like you, O Lord,
nor work to compare with yours.

All the nations shall come to adore you
and glorify your name, O Lord,
for you are great and do marvelous deeds,
you who alone are God.

from Psalm 86

Paul wrote: The word is near you, on your lips and in your heart (that is, the word of faith that we proclaim); because if you confess with your lips that Jesus is Lord and believe in your heart that God raised him from the dead, you will be saved. For one believes with the heart and so is justified, and one confesses with the mouth and so is saved. The scripture says, "No one who believes in him will be put to shame." For there is no distinction between Jew and Greek; the same Lord is Lord of all and is generous to all who call on him. For "everyone who calls on the name of the Lord shall be saved."

Romans 10,8-13

or

Jesus, full of the Holy Spirit, returned from the Jordan and was led by the Spirit in the wilderness, where for forty days he was tempted by the devil. He ate nothing at all during those days, and when they were over, he was famished. The devil said to him, "If you are the Son of God, command this stone to become a loaf of bread." Jesus answered him, "It is written, 'One does not live by bread alone.'" Then the devil led him up and showed him in an instant all the kingdoms of the world. And the devil said to him, "To you I will give their glory and all this authority; for it has been given over to me, and I give it to anyone I please. If you, then, will worship me, it will all be yours." Jesus answered him, "It is written, 'Worship the Lord your God, and serve only him.'" Then the devil took him to Jerusalem, and placed him on pinnacle of the temple, saying to him, "If you are the Son of God, throw yourself down from here, for it is written, 'He will command his angels concerning you, to protect you,' and 'On their hands they will bear you up, so that you will not dash your foot against a stone.'" Jesus answered him, "It is said, 'Do not put the Lord your God to the test.'" When the devil had finished every test, he departed from him until an opportune time.

Luke 4,1-13

SONG

SILENCE

INTERCESSIONS

Lord Christ, to whom would we go? You have the words of eternal life.
—May your word enlighten us.

Lord Christ, you tell us: You are the salt of the earth.
—May your word enlighten us.

Lord Christ, you tell us: Love your enemies.
—May your word enlighten us.

Lord Christ, you tell us: Do good to those who hate you.
—May your word enlighten us.

Lord Christ, you tell us: Be merciful.
—May your word enlighten us.

Lord Christ, you tell us: Pray, ask, seek and you will find.
—May your word enlighten us.

Lord Christ, you tell us: Seek first the Kingdom of God.
—May your word enlighten us.

OUR FATHER

PRAYER

Christ Jesus, when temptation urges us to abandon you, you pray within us. And you encourage us not to remain in darkness, but to live in your light.

or

Bless us, Risen Jesus; you offer us this Gospel freshness: to begin everything with a heart that trusts.

SONGS

Lent 5

SONG

PSALM

O Lord, you have been our refuge
from one generation to the next.

Before the mountains were born
or the earth or the world brought forth,
you are God, without beginning or end.

You turn us back into dust.
To your eyes a thousand years
are like yesterday, come and gone,
no more than a watch in the night.

Make us know the shortness of our life
that we may gain wisdom of heart.
In the morning, fill us with your love;
we shall exult and rejoice all our days.

Show forth your work to your servants;
let your glory shine on their children.
Let the favor of the Lord be upon us.

from Psalm 90

READING

The days are surely coming, says the Lord, when I will make a
new covenant with the house of Israel and the house of Judah.
It will not be like the covenant that I made with their ancestors when I took them by the hand to bring them out of the

land of Egypt–a covenant that they broke, though I was their husband, says the Lord. **But this is the covenant that I will make with the house of Israel after those days, says the Lord: I will put my law within them, and I will write it on their hearts; and I will be their God, and they shall be my people.** No longer shall they teach one another, or say to each other, "Know the Lord," for they shall all know me, from the least of them to the greatest, says the Lord; for I will forgive their iniquity, and remember their sin no more.

Jeremiah 31,31-34

or

Jesus said, "The hour has come for the Son of Man to be glorified. **Very truly, I tell you, unless a grain of wheat falls into the earth and dies, it remains just a single grain; but if it dies, it bears much fruit.** Those who love their life lose it, and those who hate their life in this world will keep it for eternal life. Whoever serves me must follow me, and where I am, there will my servant be also. Whoever serves me, the Father will honor. Now my soul is troubled. And what should I say–Father, save me from this hour? No, it is for this reason that I have come to this hour. Father, glorify your name." Then a voice came from heaven, "I have glorified it, and I will glorify it again." The crowd standing there heard it and said that it was thunder. Others said, "An angel has spoken to him." Jesus answered, "This voice has come for your sake, not for mine. Now is the judgment of this world; now the ruler of this world will be driven out. And I, when I am lifted up from the earth, will draw all people to myself."

John 12,23-32

SONG

SILENCE

LITANY OF PRAISE

O Christ, by remaining faithful till death, you show us the road to greater love.

O Christ, by taking the burden of sin upon yourself, you reveal to us the way of generosity.

O Christ, by praying for those who crucified you, you lead us to forgive without counting the cost.

O Christ, by opening paradise to the repentant thief, you awaken hope in us.

O Christ, come and help our weak faith.

O Christ, create a pure heart in us; renew and strengthen our spirit.

O Christ, your Word is near, may it live within us and protect us always.

OUR FATHER

PRAYER

Christ Jesus, even when we can feel nothing of your presence, you are always there. Your Holy Spirit remains continually active in us, opening little ways forward to escape from our dead ends and to move towards the essential of faith, of trust.

or

Bless us, Christ Jesus; though we have never seen you, we love you.

SONGS

Lent 6

SONG

PSALM

Out of the depths I cry to you, O Lord,
Lord, hear my voice!
O let your ears be attentive
to the voice of my pleading.

If you, O Lord, should mark our guilt,
Lord, who would survive?
But with you is found forgiveness:
for this we revere you.

My soul is waiting for the Lord.
I count on God's word.
My soul is longing for the Lord
more than those who watch for daybreak.

Because with the Lord there is mercy
and fullness of redemption,
Israel indeed God will redeem
from all its iniquity.

Psalm 130

READING

Thus says the Lord: Do not remember the former things, or
consider the things of old. I am about to do a new thing; now
it springs forth, do you not perceive it? I will make a way in
the wilderness and rivers in the desert. The wild animals will

honor me, the jackals and the ostriches; for I give water in the wilderness, rivers in the desert, to give drink to my chosen people, the people whom I formed for myself so that they might declare my praise.

Isaiah 43,18-21

or

Jesus came to a Samaritan city called Sychar, near the plot of ground that Jacob had given to his son Joseph. Jacob's well was there, and Jesus, tired out by his journey, was sitting by the well. It was about noon. A Samaritan woman came to draw water, and Jesus said to her, "Give me a drink." (His disciples had gone to the city to buy food.) The Samaritan woman said to him, "How is it that you, a Jew, ask a drink of me, a woman of Samaria?" (Jews do not share things in common with Samaritans.) Jesus answered her, "If you knew the gift of God, and who it is that is saying to you, Give me a drink, you would have asked him, and he would have given you living water." The woman said to him, "Sir, you have no bucket, and the well is deep. Where do you get that living water? Are you greater than our ancestor Jacob, who gave us the well, and with his sons and his flocks drank from it?" Jesus said to her, "Everyone who drinks of this water will be thirsty again, but **those who drink of the water that I will give them will never be thirsty. The water that I will give will become in them a spring of water gushing up to eternal life.**"

John 4,5-14

SONG

SILENCE

Lord Christ, reveal the presence of your Kingdom in our midst.

O God, keep watch over the gate of our lips; may every hurt of this day be buried in your forgiveness.

Lord Jesus, show your light to the hearts that can no longer find the road to you.

O Christ, by your life offered to God, show us the road to life.

O Christ, remain alongside all who are undergoing a night of torment, the ill and the homeless.

O Christ, keep us from the snares of discouragement and worry.

Our eyes are turned to you, O Lord; our soul finds rest in you.

OUR FATHER

PRAYER

Living God, at times we are strangers on the earth, disconcerted by the violence, the harsh oppositions. And you breathe upon us the Spirit of peace like a gentle breeze. Transfigure the deserts of our doubts and so prepare us to be bearers of reconciliation wherever you place us, until a hope of peace arises in our world.

or

Bless us, Christ Jesus; enable us to surrender everything to you.

SONGS

Lent 7

PSALM

Lord, make haste and answer;
for my spirit fails within me.
Do not hide your face
lest I become like those in the grave.

In the morning let me know your love
for I put my trust in you.
Make me know the way I should walk;
to you I lift up my soul.

Teach me to do your will
for you, O Lord, are my God.
Let your good spirit guide me
in ways that are level and smooth.

For your name's sake, Lord, save my life;
in your justice save my soul from distress.
Rescue my life from oppression
for I am your servant, O Lord.

from Psalm 143

READING

Paul wrote: **So we are ambassadors for Christ, since God is making his appeal through us; we entreat you on behalf of Christ, be reconciled to God.** For our sake he made him to be sin who knew no sin, so that in him we might become the righteousness of God. As we work together with him, we urge you also not to accept the grace of God in vain. For he says, "At an acceptable time I have listened to you, and on a day of salvation I have helped you." See, now is the acceptable time; see, now is the day of salvation!.

2 Corinthians 5,20 - 6,2

or

When Mary came where Jesus was and saw him, she knelt at his feet and said to him, "Lord, if you had been here, my brother would not have died." When Jesus saw her weeping, and the Jews who came with her also weeping, he was greatly disturbed in spirit and deeply moved. He said, "Where have you laid him?" They said to him, "Lord, come and see." Jesus began to weep. So the Jews said, "See how he loved him!" But some of them said, "Could not he who opened the eyes of the blind man have kept this man from dying?" Then Jesus, again greatly disturbed, came to the tomb. It was a cave, and a stone was lying against it. Jesus said, "Take away the stone." Martha, the sister of the dead man, said to him, "Lord, already there is a stench because he has been dead four days." Jesus said to her, "Did I not tell you that if you believed, you would see the glory of God?" So they took away the stone. And **Jesus looked upward and said, "Father, I thank you for having heard me. I knew that you always hear me, but I have said this for the sake of the crowd standing here, so that they may believe that you sent me." When he had said this, he cried with a loud voice, "Lazarus, come out!" The dead man came out, his hands and feet bound with strips of cloth, and his face wrapped in a cloth. Jesus said to them, "Unbind him, and let him go."**

John 11,32-44

SONG

LITANY OF PRAISE

Jesus, Son of the living God, splendor of the Father, eternal light, we worship you.

Jesus, gentle and humble of heart, our help and our refuge, we worship you.

Jesus, God of peace, friend of all, source of life and of holiness, fullness comes from you.

Jesus, brother of the poor, goodness without measure, inexhaustible wisdom, we worship you.

Jesus, good shepherd, true light, our way and our life, we worship you.

Jesus, joy of the angels, master of the apostles, strength of the martyrs, we worship you.

Jesus, light of the witnesses to the Gospel, radiance of all the saints, you satisfy our longing.

OUR FATHER

PRAYER

Breath of God's loving, in each person you place faith. It is a simple trust, so simple that all can welcome it. Recognized or not, you kindle a fire in our darkness that never dies out.

Bless us, Christ Jesus; your forgiveness and your presence bring to birth trust and praise in us.

SONGS

Holy Week   1

PSALM

My God, my God, why have you forsaken me?
You are far from my plea and the cry of my distress.
O my God, I call by day and you give no reply;
I call by night and I find no peace.

Yet you, O God, are holy,
enthroned on the praises of Israel.
In you our forebears put their trust;
they trusted and you set them free.
When they cried to you, they escaped.
In you they trusted and never in vain.

But I am a worm and no man,
the butt of all, laughing-stock of the people.
All who see me deride me.
They curl their lips, they toss their heads.
"He trusted in the Lord, let him save him,
and release him if this is his friend."

Yes, it was you who took me from the womb,
entrusted me to my mother's breast.
To you I was committed from my birth,
from my mother's womb you have been my God.
Do not leave me alone in my distress
Come close, there is none else to help.

from Psalm 22

READING

For he grew up before him like a young plant, and like a root out of dry ground; he had no form or majesty that we should look at him, nothing in his appearance that we should desire him. He was despised and rejected by others; a man of suffering and acquainted with infirmity; and as one from whom others hide their faces he was despised, and we held him of no account. Surely he has borne our infirmities and carried our diseases; yet we accounted him stricken, struck down by God, and afflicted. But he was wounded for our transgressions, crushed for our iniquities; upon him was the punishment that made us whole, and by his bruises we are healed.

Isaiah 53,2-5

or

While they were eating, Jesus took a loaf of bread, and after blessing it he broke it, gave it to the disciples, and said, "Take, eat; this is my body." Then he took a cup, and after giving thanks he gave it to them, saying, "Drink from it, all of you; for this is my blood of the covenant, which is poured out for many for the forgiveness of sins. I tell you, I will never again drink of this fruit of the vine until that day when I drink it new with you in my Father's kingdom."

Matthew 26,26-29

SONG

SILENCE

LITANY OF PRAISE

O Christ Savior, like the seed fallen to the ground, you suffered death. United to you, our life will bear much fruit.
–We praise you, Lord!

O Christ, you went down to the lowest point of the human condition; you remain close to all who are abandoned.
–We praise you, Lord!

In your love you took upon yourself our sins; innocent, you accepted death to free us from death.
–We praise you, Lord!

By your love you conquered evil and hatred, and you live for ever at the Father's side.
–We praise you, Lord!

You listen to us in your goodness and you visit us in our misfortune; fill our hearts to overflowing by revealing to us the light of your face.
–We praise you, Lord!

OUR FATHER

PRAYER

O Christ, you give everything, you give your life and also your forgiveness; it will never vanish. And we stammer our response: Christ, you know that I love you. Perhaps not as I would like to, but I do love you.

or

Jesus, joy of our hearts, you remain alongside us like someone who is poor and also as the Risen Lord. You want to turn us into people who are fully alive, not lukewarm. And every time a distance opens up between ourselves and you, you invite us to follow you by remaining close beside you.

or

Bless us, Christ Jesus; when threatened you did not retaliate, and you come to heal us by your compassion.

SONGS

Holy Week   2

PSALM

With all my voice I cry to you, Lord,
with all my voice I entreat you, Lord.
I pour out my trouble before you;
I tell you all my distress
while my spirit faints within me.
But you, O Lord, know my path.

On the way where I shall walk
they have hidden a snare to entrap me.
Look on my right and see:
there is no one who takes my part.
I have no means of escape,
not one who cares for my soul.

I cry to you, O Lord,
I have said, "You are my refuge,
all I have in the land of the living."
Listen, then, to my cry
for I am in the depths of distress.

Rescue me from those who pursue me
for they are stronger than I.
Bring my soul out of this prison
and then I shall praise your name.
Around me the just will assemble
because of your goodness to me.

Psalm 142

READING

Paul wrote: Let the same mind be in you that was in Christ Jesus, who, though he was in the form of God, did not regard equality with God as something to be exploited, but emptied himself, taking the form of a slave, being born in human like-ness. And being found in human form, he humbled himself and became obedient to the point of death—even death on a cross. Therefore God also highly exalted him and gave him the name that is above every name, so that at the name of Jesus every knee should bend, in heaven and on earth and under the earth, and every tongue should confess that Jesus Christ is Lord, to the glory of God the Father.

Philippians 2,5-11

or

Now before the festival of the Passover, Jesus knew that his hour had come to depart from this world and go to the Father. Having loved his own who were in the world, he loved them to the end. (...) During supper Jesus, knowing that the Father had given all things into his hands, and that he had come from God and was going to God, **got up from the table, took off his outer robe, and tied a towel around him-self. Then he poured water into a basin and began to wash the disciples' feet and to wipe them with the towel that was tied around him.** (...) After he had washed their feet, had put on his robe, and had returned to the table, he said to them, "Do you know what I have done to you? You call me Teacher and Lord—and you are right, for that is what I am. So if I, your Lord and Teacher, have washed your feet, you also ought to wash one another's feet. For I have set you an example, that you also should do as I have done to you."

John 13,1.3-5.12-15

SONG

SILENCE

LITANY OF PRAISE

Let us contemplate Jesus the Lord: instead of the joy meant for him, he endured the cross, disregarding its disgrace.
–We worship you, Lord, upon the cross.

O Jesus Christ, born in humility to confound the proud and to raise the humble,
–We worship you, Lord, upon the cross.

You lived among us, healing the sick, proclaiming Good News to the poor and freedom to prisoners.
–We worship you, Lord, upon the cross.

You came to unbind the chains of every slavery, friend of the humble, bread of hungry hearts,
–We worship you, Lord, upon the cross.

Jesus, full of patience and goodness, you showed forgiveness and kindness to the very end.
–We worship you, Lord, upon the cross.

Jesus, gentle and humble of heart, you call to yourself all who are weary and burdened.
–We worship you, Lord, upon the cross.

Jesus, you came into the world to serve and to give your life; you were betrayed for money, dragged before judges and nailed to the cross.
–We worship you, Lord, upon the cross.

Jesus, Lord of the universe, by your resurrection from the dead you are alive at the Father's side and there you prepare a place for us.
–We worship you, Lord, upon the cross.

OUR FATHER

PRAYER

God of all loving, you always welcome us. Why should we wait for our hearts to be changed in order to live for you? You offer all we need to soothe and heal our wounds.

or

Bless us, Lord Christ; you burn away the trials of life in the fire of your presence.

SONGS

Holy Week   3

PSALM

I love the Lord, for the Lord has heard
the cry of my appeal.
The Lord was attentive to me
on the day when I called.

They surrounded me, the snares of death,
with the anguish of the tomb;
they caught me, sorrow and distress.
I called on the Lord's name.

How gracious is the Lord, and just,
our God has compassion.
The Lord protects the simple hearts;
I was helpless so God saved me.

Turn back, my soul, to your rest
for the Lord has been good,
and has kept my soul from death,
my feet from stumbling.

I will walk in the presence of the Lord
in the land of the living.

Psalm 116

READING

I know that my Redeemer lives, and that at the last he will

stand upon the earth; and after my skin has been thus destroyed, then in my flesh I shall see God, whom I shall see on my side, and my eyes shall behold, and not another. My heart faints within me!

Job 19,25-27

or

When they came to the place that is called The Skull, they crucified Jesus there with the criminals, one on his right and one on his left. Then Jesus said, "Father, forgive them; for they do not know what they are doing." And they cast lots to divide his clothing. And the people stood by, watching; but the leaders scoffed at him, saying, "He saved others; let him save himself if he is the Messiah of God, his chosen one!" The soldiers also mocked him, coming up and offering him sour wine, and saying, "If you are the King of the Jews, save yourself!" There was also an inscription over him, "This is the King of the Jews." One of the criminals who were hanged there kept deriding him and saying, "Are you not the Messiah? Save yourself and us!" But the other rebuked him, saying, "Do you not fear God, since you are under the same sentence of condemnation? And we indeed have been condemned justly, for we are getting what we deserve for our deeds, but this man has done nothing wrong." Then he said, "Jesus, remember when you come into your kingdom." He replied, "Truly I tell you, today you will be with me in Paradise." **It was now about noon, and darkness came over the whole land until three in the afternoon, while the sun's light failed; and the curtain of the temple was torn in two. Then Jesus, crying with a loud voice, said, "Father, into your hands I commend my spirit." Having said this, he breathed his last.**

Luke 23,33-46

SONG

INTERCESSIONS

O Christ, your life was no triumph, you carried a cross; may we walk along the same road as you.

O Christ, by your suffering you learned faithfulness; you became a source of eternal salvation for the whole human race.

O Christ, when threatened you did not retaliate; enable us to forgive to the very end.

O Christ, you see the pain of those who are exiled and abandoned; take their suffering upon yourself.

O Christ, when lies and worries try to separate us from you, your Holy Spirit is always with us.

O Christ, you are the happiness of those who follow you: enable us to live by your trust.

O Christ, our life is hidden with you in God; that is a joy that touches the depths of the soul.

OUR FATHER

PRAYER

God of every human being, in a world where we are bewildered by the incomprehensible suffering of the innocent, how can we be witnesses to the Gospel? Enable us to manifest a reflection of the compassion of Christ by the lives that we live.

or

Strengthen us, Eternal God, and we will wait in silence and peace until the light of the Resurrection rises upon us.

or

Christ Jesus, you did not come to earth to judge the world but so that through you, the Risen Lord, every human being might be saved, reconciled. And when the love that forgives burns with a Gospel flame, the heart, even when beset by trials, can begin to live again.

SONGS

Easter and Pentecost

The week following the Easter vigil forms a single great feast of the Resurrection. Ascension Day reminds us that Christ, lifted up to the Father's side, makes us his witnesses on earth. Pentecost, fifty days after Easter, celebrates the gift of the Holy Spirit, the fulfillment of all God's promises and a new presence of God in the Church and in each one of us.

Easter 1

PSALM

Give thanks to the Lord who is good,
for God's love endures forever.

I called to the Lord in my distress;
God answered and freed me.
The Lord is at my side; I do not fear.

It is better to take refuge in the Lord
than to trust in mortals;
it is better to take refuge in the Lord
than to trust in rulers.

I was thrust down, thrust down and falling,
but the Lord was my helper.
The Lord is my strength and my song;
and has been my savior.
There are shouts of joy and victory
in the tents of the just.

The Lord's right hand has triumphed;
God's right hand raised me.
I shall not die, I shall live
and recount God's deeds.

from Psalm 118

READING

Paul wrote: If you have been raised with Christ, seek the things that are above, where Christ is, seated at the right hand of God. Set your minds on things that are above, not on things that are on earth, for you have died, and your life is hidden with Christ in God. When Christ who is your life is revealed, then you also will be revealed with him in glory.

Colossians 3,1-4

or

Early on the first day of the week, while it was still dark, Mary Magdalene came to the tomb and saw that the stone had been removed from the tomb. So she ran and went to Simon Peter and the other disciple, the one whom Jesus loved, and said to them, "They have taken the Lord out of the tomb, and we do not know where they have laid him." Then **Peter and the other disciple set out and went toward the tomb. The two were running together, but the other disciple outran Peter and reached the tomb first. He bent down to look in and saw the linen wrappings lying there, but he did not go in. Then Simon Peter came, following him, and went into the tomb. He saw the linen wrappings lying there, and the cloth that had been on Jesus' head, not lying with the linen wrappings but rolled up in a place by itself. Then the other disciple, who reached the tomb first, also went in, and he saw and believed;** for as yet they did not understand the scripture, that he must rise from the dead. Then the disciples returned to their homes.

John 20,1-10

SONG

SILENCE

We worship you, Jesus our Savior; you conquered death by your cross:

You are the stone rejected by the builders; you have become the cornerstone: make all of us living stones in your Church.

We pray to you for Christians: may they live in the joy of the resurrection, and may they be a visible sign of your presence by their mutual love.

We pray to you for the leaders of your Church: as they celebrate your resurrection with all your servants, may they be strengthened for your service.

We pray to you for the leaders of the nations: may they exercise their office as servants of justice and peace.

We pray to you for all who are suffering from illness, grief, old age and exile: may your resurrection be a source of comfort and aid for them.

OUR FATHER

PRAYER

Risen Jesus, sometimes our heart calls out to you: I am not worthy to receive you, but only say the word and I will be healed. At the core of our life your Gospel is light within us, your Eucharist is a presence within us.

or

Jesus our joy, in your presence we find forgiveness, the clear flowing waters. Thirsting for the realities of God, we recognize your presence as the Risen Lord. And just as the almond tree begins to blossom in the light of springtime, you make even the deserts of the soul burst into flower.

SONGS

Easter 2

SONG

PSALM

You are my praise in the great assembly.
My vows I will pay before those who fear God.
The poor shall eat and shall have their fill.
Those who seek the Lord shall praise the Lord
May their hearts live for ever and ever!

All the earth shall remember and shall return to the Lord,
all families of the nations shall bow down in awe;
for the kingdom is the Lord's, who is ruler of all.
They shall bow down in awe, all the mighty of the earth,
all who must die and go down to the dust.

My soul shall live for God and my children too shall serve.
They shall tell of the Lord to generations yet to come;
declare to those unborn, the faithfulness of God.
"These things the Lord has done!"

from Psalm 22

READING

The Lord says: "Listen! I am standing at the door, knocking; if
you hear my voice and open the door, I will come in to you and
eat with you, and you with me."

Revelation 3,20

or

When it was evening on that day, the first day of the week, and the doors of the house where the disciples had met were locked for fear of the Jews, Jesus came and stood among them and said, "Peace be with you." After he said this, he showed them his hands and his side. Then the disciples rejoiced when they saw the Lord. Jesus said to them again, "Peace be with you. As the Father has sent me, so I send you." When he had said this, he breathed on them and said to them, "Receive the Holy Spirit. If you forgive the sins of any, they are forgiven them."

John 20,19-23a

SONG

SILENCE

INTERCESSIONS

O Christ, by your resurrection you open to all people the gates of the Kingdom: lead us to the Father's glory.

By your resurrection you strengthened the faith of your disciples and you sent them into the world: may your Church be faithful in turn in proclaiming the Good News.

By your resurrection you reconciled us in your peace: enable all the baptized to enter into one and the same communion of faith and love.

By your resurrection you heal our humanity and you give us eternal life: we entrust all the sick to you.

By your resurrection you have become the first of the living.

OUR FATHER

PRAYER

Risen Jesus, you breathe your Holy Spirit upon us. And we would like to say to you: you have the words that give life to our soul; to whom else would we go but to you, the Risen Lord?

SONGS

Easter 3

SONG

PSALM

Sing a new song to the Lord,
sing praise in the assembly of the faithful.
Let Israel rejoice in its maker,
let Zion's people exult in their king.

Let them praise God's name with dancing
and make music with timbrel and harp
For the Lord takes delight in his people,
and crowns the poor with salvation.

Let the faithful rejoice in their glory,
shout for joy and take their rest.
Let the praise of God be on their lips...
This honor is for all God's people.

from Psalm 149

READING

Paul wrote: I handed on to you as of first importance what I in
turn had received: that Christ died for our sins in accordance
with the scriptures, and that he was buried, and that he was
raised on the third day in accordance with the scriptures, and
that he appeared to Cephas, then to the twelve.

1 Corinthians 15,3-5

or

On the day of Jesus' resurrection, two of his disciples were going to a village called Emmaus, about seven miles from Jerusalem, and talking with each other about all these things that had happened. While they were talking and discussing, Jesus himself came near and went with them, but their eyes were kept from recognizing him. (...) And he said to them, "Was it not necessary that the Messiah should suffer these things and then enter into his glory?" Then beginning with Moses and all the prophets, he interpreted to them the things about himself in all the scriptures. As they came near the village to which they were going, he walked ahead as if he were going on. But they urged him strongly, saying, "Stay with us, because it is almost evening and the day is now nearly over." So he went in to stay with them. **When he was at the table with them, he took bread, blessed and broke it, and gave it to them. Then their eyes were opened, and they recognized him; and he vanished from their sight. They said to each other, "Were not our hearts burning within us while he was talking to us on the road, while he was opening the scriptures to us?"**

Luke 24,13-16.26-32

SONG

SILENCE

INTERCESSIONS

O Christ, born of the Father before all ages, you took upon yourself our humanity and you rose for us: we worship you.
–Glory to you, O Lord.

Son of God, Source of life, we invoke your goodness upon us and upon the entire human family.
–Hear us, Lord of glory.

Allow us to live by your life and walk as children of light in the joy of Easter.
–Hear us, Lord of glory.

Increase the faith of your Church; may it faithfully bear witness to your resurrection.
–Hear us, Lord of glory.

Comfort all who are burdened, and engrave in their hearts your words of eternal life.
–Hear us, Lord of glory.

Strengthen those who are weak in faith, and reveal yourself to doubting hearts.
–Hear us, Lord of glory.

Give strength to the sick, support the elderly and reassure the dying by your saving presence.
–Hear us, Lord of glory.

OUR FATHER

PRAYER

Risen Christ, through the Gospel your voice makes itself heard softly. You tell us: "Why worry? Only one thing is necessary, a heart attentive to my words and to the Holy Spirit."

SONGS

Easter 4

SONG

PSALM

I love you, Lord, my strength,
my rock, my fortress, my savior.
God, you are the rock where I take refuge;
my shield, my mighty help, my stronghold.

Lord, you are worthy of all praise,
when I call I am saved from my foes.
The snares of the grave entangled me;
the traps of death confronted me.

In my anguish I called to you, Lord;
I cried to you, God, for help.
From your temple you heard my voice;
my cry came to your ears.

They assailed me in the day of my misfortune,
but you, Lord, were my support.
You brought me forth into freedom,
you saved me because you loved me.

from Psalm 18

READING

John wrote: Everyone who believes that Jesus is the Christ has
been born of God, and everyone who loves the parent loves the
child. By this we know that we love the children of God, when
we love God and obey his commandments. For the love of God

is this, that we obey his commandments. And his commandments are not burdensome, for whatever is born of God conquers the world. And this is the victory that conquers the world, our faith.

1 John 5,1-4

or

Thomas (who was called the Twin), one of the twelve, was not with them when Jesus came. So the other disciples told him, "We have seen the Lord." But he said to them, "Unless I see the mark of the nails in his hands, and put my finger in the mark of the nails and my hand in his side, I will not believe." A week later his disciples were again in the house, and Thomas was with them. Although the doors were shut, Jesus came and stood among them and said, "Peace be with you." Then he said to Thomas, "Put your finger here and see my hands. Reach out your hand and put it in my side. Do not doubt but believe." Thomas answered him, "My Lord and my God!" Jesus said to him, "Have you believed because you have seen me? Blessed are those who have not seen and yet have come to believe."

John 20,24-29

SONG

SILENCE

INTERCESSIONS

O Risen Christ, your heart exults and your soul rejoices: comfort all who are living in sorrow.

Risen Lord, you come to transfigure our being: kindle in us the fire of your love.

Risen Lord, in you our resurrection has already begun on this earth: kindle in us the fire of your love.

Risen Lord, you come to fill our hearts with peace: kindle in us the fire of your love.

Risen Lord, your Spirit burns away sadness in us: kindle in us the fire of your love.

Risen Lord, you come to gather us in your Body, the Church: kindle in us the fire of your love.

OUR FATHER

PRAYER

Risen Christ, when we have the simple desire to welcome your love, little by little a flame is kindled in the depths of our being. Fueled by the Holy Spirit, this flame of love may be quite faint at first. The amazing thing is that it keeps on burning. And when we realize that you love us, the trust of faith becomes our own song.

SONGS

Easter 5

PSALM

Lord, you are my shepherd;
there is nothing I shall want.
Fresh and green are the pastures
where you give me repose.
Near restful waters you lead me,
to revive my drooping spirit.

You guide me along the right path;
you are true to your name.
If I should walk in the valley of darkness
no evil would I fear.
You are there with your crook and your staff;
with these you give me comfort.

You have prepared a banquet for me
in the sight of my foes.
My head you have anointed with oil;
my cup is overflowing.

Surely goodness and kindness shall follow me
all the days of my life.
In the Lord's own house shall I dwell
for ever and ever.

Psalm 23

READING

Christ suffered for you, leaving you an example, so that you should follow in his steps. "He committed no sin, and no deceit was found in his mouth." When he was abused, he did not return abuse; when he suffered, he did not threaten; but he entrusted himself to the one who judges justly.

1 Peter 2,21-23

or

Jesus said, "I am the good shepherd. The good shepherd lays down his life for the sheep. The hired hand, who is not the shepherd and does not own the sheep, sees the wolf coming and leaves the sheep and runs away–and the wolf snatches them and scatters them. The hired hand runs away because a hired hand does not care for the sheep. **I am the good shepherd. I know my own and my own know me, just as the Father knows me and I know the Father. And I lay down my life for the sheep.** I have other sheep that do not belong to this fold. I must bring them also, and they will listen to my voice. So there will be one flock, one shepherd. For this reason the Father loves me, because I lay down my life in order to take it up again. No one takes it from me, but I lay it down of my own accord. I have power to lay it down, and I have power to take it up again. I have received this command from my Father."

John 10,11-18

SONG

SILENCE

LITANY OF PRAISE

Risen Christ, you are alive for ever; we worship you.
–We praise you, Risen Lord!

You took the lowest place to reveal the Father's love to every human being.
–We praise you, Risen Lord!

You ascended to your Father and our Father.
–We praise you, Risen Lord!

O Christ, just as on the evening of your resurrection, you breathe your Holy Spirit upon each one of us.
–We praise you, Risen Lord!

You make us witnesses to your presence.
–We praise you, Risen Lord!

OUR FATHER

PRAYER

Jesus, Love of all loving, your compassion is without limit. We are thirsting for you, the one who tells us: "Why be afraid? Have no fear; I am here."

SONGS

Easter 6

PSALM

Preserve me, God, I take refuge in you.
I say to you Lord: "You are my God.
My happiness lies in you alone."

O Lord, it is you who are my portion and cup,
it is you yourself who are my prize.
The lot marked out for me is my delight,
welcome indeed is the heritage that falls to me!

I will bless you, Lord, you give me counsel,
and even at night direct my heart.
I keep you, Lord, ever in my sight;
since you are at my right hand, I shall stand firm.

And so my heart rejoices, my soul is glad;
even my body shall rest in safety.
For you will not leave my soul among the dead,
nor let your beloved know decay.

You will show me the path of life,
the fullness of joy in your presence,
at your right hand happiness for ever.

from Psalm 16

READING

Come to him, a living stone, though rejected by mortals yet chosen and precious in God's sight, and like living stones, let yourselves be built into a spiritual house, to be a holy priesthood, to offer spiritual sacrifices acceptable to God through Jesus Christ. (...) You are a chosen race, a royal priesthood, a holy nation, God's own people, in order that you may proclaim the mighty acts of him who called you out of darkness into his marvelous light. Once you were not a people, but now you are God's people; once you had not received mercy, but now you have received mercy.

1 Peter 2,4-5.9-10

or

Jesus said, "Do not let your hearts be troubled. Believe in God, believe also in me. In my Father's house there are many dwelling places. If it were not so, would I have told you that I go to prepare a place for you? And if I go and prepare a place for you, I will come again and will take you to myself, so that where I am, there you may be also. And you know the way to the place where I am going." Thomas said to him, "Lord, we do not know where you are going. How can we know the way?" Jesus said to him, **"I am the way, and the truth, and the life. No one comes to the Father except through me."**

John 14,1-6

SONG

SILENCE

INTERCESSIONS

O Christ, you sent the Holy Spirit received from the Father upon your disciples: lead us by that same Spirit.

O Christ, you send us to proclaim your forgiveness: reveal your love to every human being.

O Christ, you promised that the Spirit would teach us all things: enlighten our faith.

O Christ, you promised us the Spirit of peace: renew the earth by your peace.

O Christ, you promised to send the Spirit of truth: enable us to know your love which is beyond all knowledge.

O Christ, your Spirit fills the universe, dwelling within each of us.

OUR FATHER

PRAYER

Savior of every life, in following you we choose to love and never to harden our hearts. You wish us to know a Gospel joy. And when the depths of our being are covered by a dark cloud, one way forward remains open, the way of serene trust.

SONGS

Easter 7

SONG

PSALM

Cry out with joy to the Lord, all the earth.
Serve the Lord with gladness.
Come before God, singing for joy.

Know that the Lord is God,
our Maker, to whom we belong.
We are God's people, sheep of the flock.

Enter the gates with thanksgiving,
God's courts with songs of praise.
Give thanks to God and bless his name.

Indeed, how good is the Lord,
whose merciful love is eternal;
whose faithfulness lasts forever.

Psalm 100

READING

After his suffering Jesus presented himself alive to his disciples
by many convincing proofs, appearing to them during forty
days and speaking about the kingdom of God. (...) When they
had come together, they asked him, "Lord, is this the time
when you will restore the kingdom to Israel?" He replied, "It is
not for you to know the times or periods that the Father has set
by his own authority. But you will receive power when the
Holy Spirit has come upon you; and you will be my witnesses

in Jerusalem, in all Judea and Samaria, and to the ends of the earth." When he had said this, as they were watching, he was lifted up, and a cloud took him out of their sight.

Acts 1,3b.6-9

or

Before leaving this world and going to the Father, Jesus prayed, "I ask not only on behalf of these, but also on behalf of those who will believe in me through their word, that they may all be one. As you, Father, are in me and I am in you, may they also be in us, so that the world may believe that you have sent me. The glory that you have given me I have given them, so that they may be one, as we are one, I in them and you in me, that they may become completely one, so that the world may know that you have sent me and have loved them even as you have loved me. **Father, I desire that those also, whom you have given me, may be with me where I am, to see my glory, which you have given me because you loved me before the foundation of the world. Righteous Father, the world does not know you, but I know you; and these know that you have sent me. I made your name known to them, and I will make it known, so that the love with which you have loved me may be in them, and I in them.**"

John 17,20-26

SONG

SILENCE

INTERCESSIONS

Lord Jesus, after having given your life on the cross, you entered the glory of the Father. Allow all people to share in your risen life.

In you, Jesus, God made a new covenant with us. You are with us always, until the end of time.

Jesus, you appeared to your disciples after your passion. Strengthen our faith by your presence in our midst.

Jesus, you promised the Holy Spirit to the apostles. May the Spirit of consolation renew our faithfulness to you.

Jesus, you sent your apostles to proclaim Good News to the ends of the earth. May the Holy Spirit make us witnesses to your love.

OUR FATHER

PRAYER

Lord Christ, even though we had faith enough to move mountains, without love what would we be? You love us. Without your Spirit alive in our hearts, what would we be? You love us. Taking everything upon yourself, you open for us a road to faith, to trust in God, who wants neither suffering nor human distress. Spirit of Christ, Spirit of compassion, Spirit of praise, your love for each one of us will never disappear.

SONGS

Pentecost 1

SONG

PSALM

Praise, O servants of the Lord,
praise the name of the Lord!
May the name of the Lord be blessed
both now and for evermore!
From the rising of the sun to its setting
praised be the name of the Lord!

High above all nations is the Lord,
above the heavens God's glory.
Who is like the Lord, our God,
the one enthroned on high,
who stoops from the heights to look down,
to look down upon heaven and earth?

From the dust God lifts up the lowly,
from the dungheap God raises the poor
to set them in the company of rulers,
yes, with the rulers of the people.
To the childless wife God gives a home
and gladdens her heart with children.

Psalm 113

READING

When the day of Pentecost had come, they were all together
in one place. And suddenly from heaven there came a sound
like the rush of a violent wind, and it filled the entire house

where they were sitting. Divided tongues, as of fire, appeared among them, and a tongue rested on each of them. All of them were filled with the Holy Spirit and began to speak in other languages, as the Spirit gave them ability. Now there were devout Jews from every nation under heaven living in Jerusalem. And at this sound the crowd gathered and was bewildered, because each one heard them speaking in the native language of each. (...) Peter, standing with the eleven, raised his voice and addressed them, "Men of Judea and all who live in Jerusalem, let this be known to you, and listen to what I say. Indeed, these are not drunk, as you suppose, for it is only nine o'clock in the morning. No, this is what was spoken through the prophet Joel: In the last days it will be, God declares, that I will pour out my Spirit upon all flesh, and your sons and your daughters shall prophesy, and your young men shall see visions, and your old men shall dream dreams. (...) Then everyone who calls on the name of the Lord shall be saved."

Acts 2,1-6.14-17.21

or

Jesus said, "If you love me, you will keep my commandments. And I will ask the Father, and he will give you another Advocate, to be with you forever. This is the Spirit of truth, whom the world cannot receive, because it neither sees him nor knows him. You know him, because he abides with you, and he will be in you. I will not leave you orphaned; I am coming to you. In a little while the world will no longer see me, but you will see me; because I live, you also will live. On that day you will know that I am in my Father, and you in me, and I in you."

John 14,15-20

SONG

INTERCESSIONS

Come, Holy Spirit, from heaven shine forth with your radiant love.

Come, Father of the poor; come, generous Spirit; come, Light of our hearts.

Perfect Comforter, you make peace to dwell in our soul: Come, Holy Spirit.

Wonderful refreshment, in our labor you offer rest; in our trials, strength: Come, Holy Spirit.

Kindly Light, enter the inmost depth of our hearts: Come, Holy Spirit.

Bend our rigidity, inflame our apathy: Come, Holy Spirit.

Send rain upon our dry ground, heal our wounded souls: Come, Holy Spirit.

Give us lasting joy: Come Holy Spirit, from heaven shine forth with your radiant love.

OUR FATHER

PRAYER

Holy Spirit, in every situation we would like to welcome you with great simplicity. And it is above all by the intelligence of the heart that you enable us to penetrate the mystery of your life within us.

or

May the fire of Christ's love fill us, that love with which he loved us first.

SONGS

Pentecost 2

PSALM

Ring out your joy to the Lord, O you just:
for praise is fitting for loyal hearts.

Give thanks to the Lord upon the harp,
with a ten-stringed lute play your songs.
Sing to the Lord a song that is new,
play loudly, with all your skill.

For the word of the Lord is faithful
and all his works done in truth.
The Lord loves justice and right
and fills the earth with love.

By God's word the heavens were made,
by the breath of his mouth all the stars.
God collects the waves of the ocean;
and stores up the depths of the sea.

The Lord foils the designs of the nations,
and defeats the plans of the peoples.
The counsel of the Lord stands forever,
the plans of God's heart from age to age.

from Psalm 33

Paul wrote: Now there are varieties of gifts, but the same Spirit; and there are varieties of services, but the same Lord; and there are varieties of activities, but it is the same God who activates all of them in everyone. To each is given the manifestation of the Spirit for the common good.(...) For just as the body is one and has many members, and all the members of the body, though many, are one body, so it is with Christ. For in the one Spirit we were all baptized into one body–Jews or Greeks, slaves or free–and we were all made to drink of one Spirit.

1 Corinthians 12,4-7.12-13

or

Jesus said, "Those who love me will keep my word, and my Father will love them, and we will come to them and make our home with them. (...) I have said these things to you while I am still with you. But the Advocate, the Holy Spirit, whom the Father will send in my name, will teach you everything, and remind you of all that I have said to you. Peace I leave with you; my peace I give to you. I do not give to you as the world gives. Do not let your hearts be troubled, and do not let them be afraid."

John 14,23.25-27

SONG

SILENCE

INTERCESSIONS

Lord, make our lives a temple of the Holy Spirit.

Grant each of us the fruits of the Spirit: love, joy, peace, patience, kindness, faithfulness.

May the Holy Spirit speak through the lips of your servants who proclaim your Word.

Send your comforting Spirit to all who are in trouble and distress.

Send your comforting Spirit to all who are victims of injustice.

Keep all nations from hatred and war.

Gather together all the nations by the breath of your Spirit.

OUR FATHER

PRAYER

Holy Spirit, in you we find the consolation with which Christ can flood our lives. Your presence is offered to each person—and we sense that the essential has already been accomplished in us.

or

Bless us, Christ; you liberate us from isolation by the mystery of communion in your Body, the Church.

SONGS

Pentecost 3

PSALM

They are happy, whose God is the Lord,
the people who are chosen as his own.
From the heavens the Lord looks forth
and sees all the peoples of the earth.

The Lord looks on those who fear him,
on those who hope in his love,
to rescue their souls from death,
to keep them alive in famine.

Our soul is waiting for the Lord.
The Lord is our help and our shield.
Our hearts find joy in the Lord.
We trust in God's holy name.

May your love be upon us, O Lord,
as we place all our hope in you.

from Psalm 33

READING

I will sanctify my great name, which has been profaned
among the nations, and which you have profaned among
them; and the nations shall know that I am the Lord, says
the Lord God, when through you I display my holiness
before their eyes.(...) A new heart I will give you, and a new
spirit I will put within you; and I will remove from your body

122

the heart of stone and give you a heart of flesh. I will put my spirit within you, and make you follow my statutes and be careful to observe my ordinances. Then you shall live in the land that I gave to your ancestors; and you shall be my people, and I will be your God.

Ezekiel 36,23b.26-28

or

Jesus said, "I still have many things to say to you, but you cannot bear them now. **When the Spirit of truth comes, he will guide you into all the truth;** for he will not speak on his own, but will speak whatever he hears, and he will declare to you the things that are to come. He will glorify me, because he will take what is mine and declare it to you. All that the Father has is mine. For this reason I said that he will take what is mine and declare it to you."

John 16,12-15

SONG

SILENCE

LITANY OF PRAISE

Holy Spirit, Creator, In the beginning you moved over the waters. Holy Spirit, come!

Holy Spirit, Creator, from your breath all creatures drew their life.

Holy Spirit, Counselor, by your inspiration the prophets bore witness to the Word of God.

Holy Spirit, you prepared the Virgin Mary to become the mother of the Lord.

Holy Spirit, you descended upon Jesus on the day of his baptism.

Holy Spirit, you led Christ into the desert; you assisted him in proclaiming the Kingdom.

Holy Spirit, Christ promised you would always be with us and in us.

Holy Spirit, you came down upon the apostles to gather them into a new communion, the Church.

Holy Spirit, Comforter, you bring us to birth as God's children.

Holy Spirit, you make us a living sign of God's presence.

Holy Spirit, you pray within us.

OUR FATHER

PRAYER

Holy Spirit, you breathe upon what is fragile. You kindle a flame of living charity and love that remains within us, still alive under the ashes. And through you, even the fears and the nights of our heart can become the dawn of a new life.

or

Bless us, God of all loving; you come to make our lives a living sign of your Christ.

SONGS

The Time of the Church

Christ came to earth at Christmas to offer every human being a communion in God. And his Church, his Body, is called to be this communion of love. The time of the Church begins after the Christmas season and continues until Lent.

Then the time of the Church begins again after Pentecost and continues until Advent. The Holy Spirit, sent at Pentecost, constantly breathes upon human beings and invites them to communion and reconciliation.

Time of the Church   I

PRAYER

How great is your name, O Lord our God,
through all the earth!
Your majesty is praised above the heavens;
on the lips of children and of babes.

When I see the heavens, the work of your hands,
the moon and the stars which you arranged,
what are we that you should keep us in mind,
mere mortals that you care for us?

You gave us power over the work of your hands,
put all things under our feet.
All of them, sheep and cattle,
yes, even the savage beasts,
birds of the air, and fish
that make their way through the waters.

How great is your name, O Lord our God,
through all the earth!

from Psalm 8

READING

Now the LORD said to Abram, "Go from your country and
your kindred and your father's house to the land that I will
show you. I will make of you a great nation, and I will bless you,
and make your name great, so that you will be a blessing. I will

bless those who bless you (...) and in you all the families of the earth shall be blessed." So Abram went, as the LORD had told him; and Lot went with him. Abram was seventy-five years old when he departed from Haran.

Genesis 12,1-4

or

When Jesus saw the crowds, he went up the mountain; and after he sat down, his disciples came to him. Then he began to speak, and taught them, saying: "Blessed are the poor in spirit, for theirs is the kingdom of heaven. Blessed are those who mourn, for they will be comforted. Blessed are the meek, for they will inherit the earth. Blessed are those who hunger and thirst for righteousness, for they will be filled. Blessed are the merciful, for they will receive mercy. Blessed are the pure in heart, for they will see God. Blessed are the peacemakers, for they will be called children of God. Blessed are those who are persecuted for righteousness' sake, for theirs is the kingdom of heaven. Blessed are you when people revile you and persecute you and utter all kinds of evil against you falsely on my account. Rejoice and be glad, for your reward is great in heaven, for in the same way they persecuted the prophets who were before you."

Matthew 5,1-12

SONG

SILENCE

INTERCESSIONS

May your peace shine among us and your love set us free, Lord, we pray.

Keep us persevering in faith and set in our hearts the desire for your Kingdom...

Guide your Church along the way of the Gospel; may your Holy Spirit keep her welcoming...

We pray for the leaders of the nations; may they have the will to promote justice and freedom...

O Christ, you have take our weaknesses upon yourself and taken charge of our illnesses; support those who are going through trials...

For those who work with the oppressed, with foreigners and with the lonely...

We entrust to you our families and friends, all who have asked for our prayers and who pray for us...

For our country, our region (village, town...), that the Christians there may be witnesses to truth and creators of unity, Lord, we pray.

OUR FATHER

PRAYER

Jesus our joy, you want us to have hearts that are simple, a kind of springtime of the heart. And then the complications of existence do not paralyze us so much. You tell us: don't worry; even if you have very little faith, I, Christ, am with you always.

or

Bless us, Christ Jesus; in you alone our hearts find rest and peace.

SONGS

Time of the Church   2

PSALM

The Lord is my light and my help;
whom shall I fear?
the Lord is the stronghold of my life;
before whom shall I shrink?

Though an army encamp against me
my heart would not fear.
Though war break out against me
even then would I trust.

There is one thing I ask of the Lord,
for this I long,
to live in the house of the Lord,
all the days of my life,
to savor the sweetness of the Lord,
to behold his temple.

For God makes me safe in his tent
in the day of evil.
God hides me in the shelter of his tent,
on a rock I am secure.

from Psalm 27

READING

We know love by this, that Jesus laid down his life for
us–and we ought to lay down our lives for one another. How

does God's love abide in anyone who has the world's goods and sees a brother or sister in need and yet refuses help? Little children, let us love, not in word or speech, but in truth and action. And by this we will know that we are from the truth and will reassure our hearts before him whenever our hearts condemn us; for God is greater than our hearts, and he knows everything.

1 John 3,16-20

or

At that time Jesus said, "I thank you, Father, Lord of heaven and earth, because you have hidden these things from the wise and the intelligent and have revealed them to infants; yes, Father, for such was your gracious will. All things have been handed over to me by my Father; and no one knows the Son except the Father, and no one knows the Father except the Son and anyone to whom the Son chooses to reveal him. **Come to me, all you that are weary and are carrying heavy burdens, and I will give you rest.** Take my yoke upon you, and learn from me; for I am gentle and humble in heart, and you will find rest for your souls. For my yoke is easy, and my burden is light."

Matthew 11,25-30

SONG

SILENCE

INTERCESSIONS

God our Father, fill our lives with your compassion; may we live in the generosity of forgiveness.

For those who cannot believe and who give their lives in the service of others, Lord, we pray.

For the Church, ferment of communion: Lord, make your light shine upon her.

O Christ, light from above, come and visit all those who are in darkness; show them the way of your love.

Support those who are going through times of difficulty and discouragement, O source of confidence and life.

Guide us by your Spirit so that we may accomplish the will of your love; give us new hearts.

OUR FATHER

PRAYER

Jesus our peace, if our lips keep silence, our heart listens to you and also speaks to you. And you say to each one of us: surrender yourself in all simplicity to the life of the Holy Spirit; for this, the little bit of faith you have is enough.

or

Bless us, Christ Jesus; your love for each one of us will never disappear.

SONGS

Time of the Church 3

SONG

PSALM

I will bless the Lord at all times,
God's praise always on my lips;
in the Lord my soul shall make its boast.
The humble shall hear and be glad.

Glorify the Lord with me.
Together let us praise God's name.
I sought the Lord and was heard;
from all my terrors set free.

Look towards God and be radiant;
let your faces not be abashed.
When the poor cry out the Lord hears them
and rescues them from all their distress.

Taste and see that the Lord is good.
They are happy who seek refuge in God.

from Psalm 34

READING

**Beloved, let us love one another, because love is from God;
everyone who loves is born of God and knows God.** Whoever
does not love does not know God, for God is love. God's love
was revealed among us in this way: God sent his only Son into
the world so that we might live through him. In this is love, not
that we loved God but that he loved us and sent his Son for the

133

forgiveness of our sins. Beloved, since God loved us so much, we also ought to love one another. No one has ever seen God; if we love one another, God lives in us, and his love is perfected in us.

1 John 4,7-12

or

Jesus said, "The kingdom of heaven is like treasure hidden in a field, which someone found and hid; then in his joy he goes and sells all that he has and buys that field. Again, the kingdom of heaven is like a merchant in search of fine pearls; on finding one pearl of great value, he went and sold all that he had and bought it."

Matthew 13,44-46

SONG

SILENCE

INTERCESSIONS

For all those who faithfully announce your Word, Lord, we pray.

Enable us to recognize your presence in our neighbors; make us attentive to the poor and the unfortunate.

Lord, we pray for those who suffer in their workplace and for those who are without work, that their dignity may be respected.

For prisoners and those forgotten by society, keep us in solidarity with their suffering, O Source of comfort, we pray.

For abandoned children, that they may find peace with those

who welcome them, Lord, we pray.

For scholars and researchers, that their work may benefit all humanity, Lord, we pray.

For those who have responsibilities in public life, that they may act with integrity and for the good of all, Lord, we pray.

OUR FATHER

PRAYER

God of all the living, enable us to surrender ourselves to you in silence and in love. Surrendering ourselves to you does not come easily to our human condition. But you intervene in the deepest recesses of our being and your will for us is the radiance of a hope.

or

Bless us, Christ Jesus; you always come to us wherever we may be.

SONGS

Time of the Church 4

PSALM

Like the deer that yearns
for running streams,
so my soul is yearning
for you, my God.

My soul is thirsting for God,
the God of my life;
when can I enter and see
the face of God?

My tears have become my bread,
by night, by day,
as I hear it said all the day long:
"Where is your God?"

Why are you cast down, my soul,
why groan within me?
Hope in God; I will praise yet again
my savior and my God.

from Psalm 42

READING

Paul wrote: What then are we to say about these things? If God is for us, who is against us? He who did not withhold his own Son, but gave him up for all of us, will he not with him also give us everything else? Who will bring any charge against

God's elect? It is God who justifies. Who is to condemn? It is Christ Jesus, who died, yes, who was raised, who is at the right hand of God, who indeed intercedes for us. Who will separate us from the love of Christ? Will hardship, or distress, or persecution, or famine, or nakedness, or peril, or sword? As it is written, For your sake we are being killed all day long; we are accounted as sheep to be slaughtered. No, in all these things we are more than conquerors through him who loved us. For **I am convinced that neither death, nor life, nor angels, nor rulers, nor things present, nor things to come, nor powers, nor height, nor depth, nor anything else in all creation, will be able to separate us from the love of God in Christ Jesus our Lord.**

Romans 8,31-39

or

Jesus went out again beside the sea; the whole crowd gathered around him, and he taught them. As he was walking along, he saw Levi son of Alphaeus sitting at the tax booth, and he said to him, "Follow me". And he got up and followed him. And as he sat at dinner in Levi's house, many tax collectors and sinners were also sitting with Jesus and his disciples–for there were many who followed him. **When the scribes of the Pharisees saw that Jesus was eating with sinners and tax collectors, they said to his disciples, "Why does he eat with tax collectors and sinners?" When Jesus heard this, he said to them, "Those who are well have no need of a physician, but those who are sick; I have come to call not the righteous but sinners."**

Mark 2,13-17

SONG

SILENCE

LITANY OF PRAISE

Jesus, gentle and humble of heart, you visit every human being to reveal the Father's love.

Jesus, goodness without end, you liberate captives, you pardon our sins.

Jesus, our rest and our refuge, your yoke is easy and your burden light.

Jesus, sent by the Father, you heal our blindness.

Jesus, living bread, you nourish our hearts by your words.

Jesus, you came to light a fire on the earth.

Jesus, risen from the dead, you share with us your joy.

Jesus, you are the Way, the Truth and the Life.

OUR FATHER

PRAYER

Jesus, light of our hearts, since you rose from the dead, you have never stopped coming to us. Whatever point we may be at, you are always waiting for us. And you tell us: Come to me, you who are

or

Bless us, Christ; keep us in the spirit of the Beatitudes: joy, simplicity, mercy.

SONGS

Time of the Church 5

PSALM

O God, you are my God, for you I long;
for you my soul is thirsting.
My body pines for you
like a dry, weary land without water.
So I gaze on you in the sanctuary
to see your strength and your glory.

For your love is better than life,
my lips will speak your praise.
So I will bless you all my life,
in your name I will lift up my hands.
My soul shall be filled as with a banquet,
my mouth shall praise you with joy.

On my bed I remember you.
On you I muse through the night
for you have been my help;
in the shadow of your wings I rejoice.
My soul clings to you;
your right hand holds me fast.

from Psalm 63

READING

**The first Christians devoted themselves to the apostles'
teaching and fellowship, to the breaking of bread and the
prayers.** Awe came upon everyone, because many wonders and

signs were being done by the apostles. All who believed were together and had all things in common; they would sell their possessions and goods and distribute the proceeds to all, as any had need. Day by day, as they spent much time together in the temple, they broke bread at home and ate their food with glad and generous hearts, praising God and having the goodwill of all the people. And day by day the Lord added to their number those who were being saved.

Acts 2,42-47

or

As Jesus went ashore, he saw a great crowd; and he had compassion for them, because they were like sheep without a shepherd; and he began to teach them many things. When it grew late, his disciples came to him and said, "This is a deserted place, and the hour is now very late; send them away so that they may go into the surrounding country and villages and buy something for themselves to eat." But he answered them, "You give them something to eat." They said to him, "Are we to go and buy two hundred denarii worth of bread, and give it to them to eat?" And he said to them, "How many loaves have you? Go and see." When they had found out, they said, "Five, and two fish." Then he ordered them to get all the people to sit down in groups on the green grass. So they sat down in groups of hundreds and of fifties. **Taking the five loaves and the two fish, Jesus looked up to heaven, and blessed and broke the loaves, and gave them to his disciples to set before the people; and he divided the two fish among them all. And all ate and were filled; and they took up twelve baskets full of broken pieces and of the fish. Those who had eaten the loaves numbered five thousand men.**

Mark 6,34-44

SONG

140

INTERCESSIONS

Let us pray for those who are beginning to know Christ: may the Lord strengthen them on their journey.

For children, for those who take care of them and awaken them to faith, Lord, we pray.

Let us pray for the ill and those who are ending their lives in loneliness: may the Lord give them the strength they need.

Let us pray for those who are condemned to prison or exile: may the Lord sustain their hope.

That the fire of your Spirit may renew our energies and enable us to welcome those who do not know you, Lord, we pray.

May your Church be constantly renewed at the table of the Word and the Eucharist, Lord, we pray.

OUR FATHER

PRAYER

God our Father, you never stop searching for all who have gone away from you. And by your forgiveness, you place on our finger the ring of the prodigal son, the ring of festival.

or

Bless us, Christ Jesus; your love is greater than our hearts.

SONGS

Time of the Church 6

PSALM

In you, O Lord, I take refuge;
let me never be put to shame.
In your justice rescue me, free me;
pay heed to me and save me.

Be a rock where I can take refuge,
a mighty stronghold to save me;
for you are my rock, my stronghold.

It is you, O Lord, who are my hope,
my trust, O Lord, since my youth.
On you I have leaned from my birth;
from my mother's womb you have been my help.
My hope has always been in you.

My fate has filled many with awe
but you are my strong refuge.
My lips are filled with your praise,
with your glory all the day long.
Do not reject me now that I am old;
when my strength fails do not forsake me.

from Psalm 71

READING

For surely I know the plans I have for you, says the Lord,
plans for your welfare and not for harm, to give you a future

with hope. Then when you call upon me and come and pray to me, I will hear you. When you search for me, you will find me; if you seek me with all your heart.

Jeremiah 29,11-13

or

As Jesus was setting out on a journey, a man ran up and knelt before him, and asked him, "Good Teacher, what must I do to inherit eternal life?" Jesus said to him, "Why do you call me good? No one is good but God alone. You know the commandments: You shall not murder; You shall not commit adultery; You shall not steal; You shall not bear false witness; You shall not defraud; Honor your father and mother." He said to him, "Teacher, I have kept all these since my youth." **Jesus, looking at him, loved him and said, "You lack one thing; go, sell what you own, and give the money to the poor, and you will have treasure in heaven; then come, follow me."** When he heard this, he was shocked and went away grieving, for he had many possessions.

Mark 10,17-22

SONG

SILENCE

INTERCESSIONS

Jesus Christ, you come to transfigure us and to renew us in the image of God: shine in our darkness.

Jesus Christ, light of our hearts, you know our thirst: lead us to the wellspring of your Gospel.

Jesus Christ, light of the world, you shine on every human being: enable us to discern your presence in each person.

Jesus Christ, friend of the poor: open in us the gates of simplicity so that we can welcome you.

Jesus Christ, gentle and humble of heart: renew in us the spirit of childhood.

Jesus Christ, you send your Church to prepare your path in the world: open for all people the gates of your Kingdom.

OUR FATHER

PRAYER

Jesus our joy, when we realize that you love us, something in us is soothed and even transformed. We ask you: what do you want from me? And by the Holy Spirit you reply: let nothing trouble you, I am praying in you, dare to give your life.

or

Christ Jesus, although we have not seen you, we love you. And still without seeing you, we place our trust in you. Bless us; we find rest in your peace.

SONGS

Time of the Church 7

SONG

PSALM

O sing a new song to the Lord,
sing to the Lord all the earth.
O sing to the Lord, bless his name.

Proclaim God's help day by day,
tell among the nations his glory
and his wonders among all the peoples.

It was the Lord who made the heavens.
His are majesty and honor and power
and splendor in his holy place.

Let the heavens rejoice and earth be glad,
let the sea and all within it thunder praise,
let the land and all it bears rejoice,
all the trees of the wood shout for joy
at the presence of the Lord who comes.

from Psalm 96

READING

The Lord says: Surely, this commandment that I am com-
manding you today is not too hard for you, nor is it too far
away. It is not in heaven, that you should say, "Who will go up
to heaven for us, and get it for us so that we may hear it and
observe it?" Neither is it beyond the sea, that you should say,
"Who will cross to the other side of the sea for us, and get it for

us so that we may hear it and observe it?" **No, the word is very near to you; it is in your mouth and in your heart for you to observe.**

Deuteronomy 30,11-14

or

Once while Jesus was standing beside the lake of Gennesaret, and the crowd was pressing in on him to hear the word of God, he saw two boats there at the shore of the lake; the fishermen had gone out of them and were washing their nets. He got into one of the boats, the one belonging to Simon, and asked him to put out a little way from the shore. Then he sat down and taught the crowds from the boat. When he had finished speaking, **Jesus said to Simon, "Put out into the deep water and let down your nets for a catch." Simon answered, "Master, we have worked all night long but have caught nothing. Yet if you say so, I will let down the nets." When they had done this, they caught so many fish that their nets were beginning to break.** So they signaled their partners in the other boat to come and help them. And they came and filled both boats, so that they began to sink. **But when Simon Peter saw it, he fell down at Jesus' knees, saying, "Go away from me, Lord, for I am a sinful man!"** For he and all who were with him were amazed at the catch of fish that they had taken; and so also were James and John, sons of Zebedee, who were partners with Simon. Then **Jesus said to Simon, "Do not be afraid; from now on you will be catching people." When they had brought their boats to shore, they left everything and followed him.**

Luke 5,1-11

SONG

SILENCE

INTERCESSIONS

For peace in the world and the liberation of all people, Lord, we pray.

That the leaders of the Churches may tirelessly seek visible unity among Christians, Lord, we pray.

For honesty in political life, for justice in society, Lord, we pray.

For those who toil to earn their daily bread, Lord, we pray.

For those without work or resources, Lord, we pray.

For those with no family or home, Lord, we pray.

For those who suffer from loneliness or abandonment, Lord, we pray.

For those who are oppressed or maligned, Lord, we pray.

For those who work with the poor, with foreigners and with the excluded, Lord, we pray.

OUR FATHER

PRAYER

Living God, however poor our prayer is, we search for you with confidence. And your love carves out a way forward through our hesitations and even through our doubts.

or

You have blessed us, living God; you bury our past in the heart of Christ and are going to take care of our future.

SONGS

Time of the Church 8

PSALM

My soul, give thanks to the Lord,
all my being, bless God's holy name.
My soul, give thanks to the Lord
and never forget all God's blessings.

It is God who forgives all your guilt,
who heals every one of your ills,
who redeems your life from the grave,
who crowns you with love and compassion,
who fills your life with good things,
renewing your youth like an eagle's.

The Lord does deeds of justice,
gives judgment to all who are oppressed.
The Lord's ways were made known to Moses;
the Lord's deeds to Israel's children.

The Lord is compassion and love,
slow to anger and rich in mercy.
God does not treat us according to our sins
nor repay us according to our faults.

For as the heavens are high above the earth
so strong is God's love for the God-fearing;
As far as the east is from the west
so far does he remove our sins.

from Psalm 103

READING

Why do you say, O Jacob, and speak, O Israel, "My way is hidden from the Lord, and my right is disregarded by my God"? Have you not known? Have you not heard? The Lord is the everlasting God, the Creator of the ends of the earth. He does not faint or grow weary; his understanding is unsearchable. He gives power to the faint, and strengthens the powerless. **Even youths will faint and be weary, and the young will fall exhausted; but those who wait for the Lord shall renew their strength, they shall mount up with wings like eagles, they shall run and not be weary, they shall walk and not faint.**

Isaiah 40,27-31

or

Jesus said, "But I say to you that listen, Love your enemies, do good to those who hate you, bless those who curse you, pray for those who abuse you. If anyone strikes you on the cheek, offer the other also; and from anyone who takes away your coat do not withhold even your shirt. Give to everyone who begs from you; and if anyone takes away your goods, do not ask for them again. Do to others as you would have them do to you. If you love those who love you, what credit is that to you? For even sinners love those who love them. (...) But **love your enemies, do good and lend expecting nothing in return. Your reward will be great, and you will be children of the Most High; for he is kind to the ungrateful and the wicked.**"

Luke 6,27-32.35

SONG

SILENCE

LITANY OF PRAISE

Lord God, you do not look at appearances but at our heart; you are forgiveness.

Lord God, you renew in us peace of heart and a serene joy.

O Risen Christ, you are with us, even with those who are unaware of your presence.

O Risen Christ, you place in our hearts a longing for your Kingdom.

O Risen Christ, you call us to share the fruits of the earth and of our work.

Lord God, by your Christ the fullness of your life is offered to us.

Lord God, into your hands we place our entire life.

OUR FATHER

PRAYER

Jesus our peace, by the Holy Spirit you always come to us. And in the deepest part of our soul, there is the wonder of a presence. Our prayer may be quite poor, but you pray within us.

or

Blessed be those who are seeking God and his Christ. Blessed be the simple-hearted according to the Gospel.

SONGS

Time of the Church   9

PSALM

I trusted, even when I said:
"I am sorely afflicted,"
and when I said in my alarm:
"There is no one I can trust."

How can I repay the Lord
for his goodness to me?
The cup of salvation I will raise;
I will call on the Lord's name.

O precious in the eyes of the Lord
is the death of the faithful.
Your servant, Lord, your servant am I;
you have loosened my bonds.

A thanksgiving sacrifice I make;
I will call on the Lord's name
I will walk in the presence of the Lord
in the land of the living.

My vows to the Lord I will fulfill
before all the people,
in the courts of the house of the Lord,
in your midst, O Jerusalem.

from Psalm 116

Jeremiah said: The word of the Lord came to me saying, "Before I formed you in the womb I knew you, and before you were born I consecrated you; I appointed you a prophet to the nations." Then I said, "Ah, Lord God! Truly I do not know how to speak, for I am only a boy." But the Lord said to me, "Do not say, 'I am only a boy'; for you shall go to all to whom I send you, and you shall speak whatever I command you, Do not be afraid of them, for I am with you to deliver you, says the Lord."

Jeremiah 1,4-8

or

Jesus said: There was a man who had two sons. The younger of them said to his father, "Father, give me the share of the property that will belong to me." So he divided his property between them. A few days later the younger son gathered all he had and traveled to a distant country, and there he squandered his property in dissolute living. When he had spent everything, a severe famine took place throughout that country, and he began to be in need. So he went and hired himself out to one of the citizens of that country, who sent him to his fields to feed the pigs. He would gladly have filled himself with the pods that the pigs were eating; and no one gave him anything. But when he came to himself he said, "How many of my father's hired hands have bread enough and to spare, but here I am dying of hunger! I will get up and go to my father, and I will say to him, 'Father, I have sinned against heaven and before you; I am no longer worthy to be called your son; treat me like one of your hired hands.'" So he set off and went to his father. But while he was still far off, his father saw him and was filled with compassion; he ran and put his arms around him and kissed him. Then the son said to him, "Father, I have sinned against heaven and before you; I am no longer worthy to be called your son." But the father said to his slaves, "Quickly, bring out a robe–the best one–and put it on him; put a ring on his finger and sandals on his feet. And get the fatted calf and kill it, and let us eat and celebrate; for this son of mine was dead and is alive again; he was lost and is found!" And they began to celebrate.

Luke 15,11-24

SONG

SILENCE

INTERCESSIONS

That Christians may never cease to go towards all people, and become ferments of reconciliation in the human family, we pray to the Lord.

For all who believe, for those who have a ministry in the Church, that they may be faithful witnesses to the Gospel, we pray to the Lord.

That the goods of the earth may be shared among all, we pray to the Lord

For all the nations of the earth, that wars and violence may cease, we pray to the Lord

For the poor and the afflicted, we pray to the Lord.

For those who are persecuted on account of Christ's name, for all who are seeking justice, we pray to the Lord.

OUR FATHER

PRAYER

Jesus, Love of all loving, you were always in me and I was forgetting you. You were in my heart of hearts and I was looking for you elsewhere. When I kept myself far from you, you were waiting for me. And now I dare to tell you: Risen Christ, you are my life.

or

Bless us, Lord Christ; by your forgiveness you place on our finger the ring of the prodigal son.

SONGS

Time of the Church   10

PSALM

I lift up my eyes to the mountains;
from where shall come my help?
My help shall come from the Lord
who made heaven and earth.

May God never allow you to stumble!
Let your guard not sleep.
Behold, neither sleeping nor slumbering,
Israel's guard.

The Lord is your guard and your shade;
and stands at your right.
By day the sun shall not smite you
nor the moon in the night.

The Lord will guard you from evil,
and will guard your soul.
The Lord will guard your going and coming
both now and for ever.

Psalm 121

READING

For we did not follow cleverly devised myths when we made
known to you the power and coming of our Lord Jesus Christ,
but we had been eyewitnesses of his majesty. For he received
honor and glory from God the Father when that voice was con-

veyed to him by the Majestic Glory, saying, "This is my Son, my Beloved, with whom I am well pleased." We ourselves heard this voice come from heaven, while we were with him on the holy mountain. So we have the prophetic message more fully confirmed. You will do well to be attentive to this as to a lamp shining in a dark place, until the day dawns and the morning star rises in your hearts.

2 Peter 1,16-19

or

Jesus entered Jericho and was passing through it. A man was there named Zacchaeus; he was a chief tax collector and was rich. He was trying to see who Jesus was, but on account of the crowd he could not, because he was short in stature. So he ran ahead and climbed a sycamore tree to see him, because he was going to pass that way. When Jesus came to the place, he looked up and said to him, "Zacchaeus, hurry and come down; for I must stay at your house today." So he hurried down and was happy to welcome him. All who saw it began to grumble and said, "He has gone to be the guest of one who is a sinner." Zacchaeus stood there and said to the Lord, "Look, half of my possessions, Lord, I will give to the poor; and if I have defrauded anyone of anything, I will pay back four times as much." Then Jesus said to him, "Today salvation has come to this house, because he too is a son of Abraham. For **the Son of Man came to seek out and to save the lost.**"

Luke 19,1-10

SONG

SILENCE

God, Creator and Savior, source of peace for the entire world: be our life today.

O Christ, you call us to share with others: unite us in your love.

O Christ, our Shepherd, you come to seek those who are lost, you visit the lonely and the abandoned: give them new hope.

Comforting Spirit, you place in us hope and joy: fill us with your love.

Comforting Spirit, you awaken in us a love that forgives: come to us, Holy Spirit.

OUR FATHER

PRAYER

Lord Christ, enable us to turn to you at every moment. So often we forget that your Holy Spirit dwells in us, that you pray in us, that you love in us. Your miracle in us is your trust, and your constant forgiveness.

or

You have blessed us, Risen Jesus; we want to root our lives in your trust, to such an extent that the wellsprings of jubilation never run dry.

SONGS

Time of the Church 11

SONG

PSALM

When the Lord delivered us from bondage,
it seemed like a dream.
Then was our mouth filled with laughter,
on our lips there were songs.

The heathens themselves said: "What marvels
the Lord worked for them!"
What marvels the Lord worked for us!
Indeed we were glad.

Deliver us, O Lord, from our bondage
as streams in dry land.
Those who are sowing in tears
will sing when they reap.

They go out, they go out, full of tears,
carrying seed for the sowing;
they come back, they come back, full of song,
carrying their sheaves.

Psalm 126

READING

Paul wrote: If I speak in the tongues of mortals and of angels, but do not have love, I am a noisy gong or a clanging cymbal. And if I have prophetic powers, and understand all mysteries and all knowledge, and if I have all faith, so as to remove mountains, but do not have love, I am nothing. If I give away all my possessions, and if I hand over my body so that I may boast, but do not have love, I gain nothing. Love is patient; love is kind; love is not envious or boastful or arrogant or rude. It does not insist on its own way; it is not irritable or resentful; it does not rejoice in wrongdoing, but rejoices in the truth. It bears all things, believes all things, hopes all things, endures all things. Love never ends. But as for prophecies, they will come to an end; as for tongues, they will cease; as for knowledge, it will come to an end. For we know only in part, and we prophesy only in part. (...) And now faith, hope, and love abide, these three; and the greatest of these is love.

I Corinthians 13,1-9.13

or

In the beginning was the Word, and the Word was with God, and the Word was God. He was in the beginning with God. All things came into being through him, and without him not one thing came into being What has come into being in him was life, and the life was the light of all people. The light shines in the darkness, and the darkness did not overcome it.

John 1,1-5

SONG

SILENCE

INTERCESSIONS

For those who are far from home, immigrants, exiles, victims of oppression, Lord, we pray.

For those who are going through trials, who need help and compassion, Lord, we pray.

For all of us gathered here, that we may remain attentive to those entrusted to us, Lord, we pray.

That we may be delivered from all anxiety, Lord, we pray.

That we may learn to share more fairly the resources of our planet among all, Lord, we pray.

That a sense of wonder at the beauty of creation may remain alive in us, Lord, we pray.

That we may find light and courage in the mystery of communion that is the Church, Lord, we pray.

OUR FATHER

PRAYER

Jesus our peace, you never abandon us. And the Holy Spirit always opens a way forward, the way which consists in casting ourselves into God as into the depths. And astonishment arises: these depths are not an abyss of darkness; they are God–fathomless depths of compassion and innocence.

or

Bless us, Lord Christ; you give peace to our hearts when the unthinkable happens, the suffering of the innocent.

SONGS

Time of the Church   12

PSALM

O Lord, you search me and you know me,
you know my resting and my rising,
you discern my purpose from afar.

You mark when I walk or lie down,
all my ways lie open to you.
Before ever a word is on my tongue
you know it, Lord, through and through.

Behind and before you besiege me,
your hand ever laid upon me.
Too wonderful for me, this knowledge,
too high, beyond my reach.

O where can I go from your spirit,
or where can I flee from your face?
If I climb the heavens, you are there.
If I lie in the grave, you are there.

If I take the wings of the dawn
and dwell at the sea's furthest end,
even there your hand would lead me,
your right hand would hold me fast.

If I say: "Let the darkness hide me
and the light around me be night,"
even darkness is not dark for you

and the night is as clear as the day.

from Psalm 139

READING

See what love the Father has given us, that we should be called children of God; and that is what we are. The reason the world does not know us is that it did not know him. Beloved, we are God's children now; what we will be has not yet been revealed. What we do know is this: when he is revealed, we will be like him, for we will see him as he is. And all who have this hope in him purify themselves, just as he is pure.

1 John 3,1-3

or

Jesus said, "God so loved the world that he gave his only Son, so that everyone who believes in him may not perish but may have eternal life. Indeed, God did not send the Son into the world to condemn the world, but in order that the world might be saved through him."

John 3,16-17

SONG

SILENCE

INTERCESSIONS

Risen Christ, you fill our lives with your compassion so that we may always seek you.

Risen Christ, you know our longing: lead us on the path of eternity.

Risen Christ, we pray to you for those who are just beginning to know you.

Risen Christ, we pray to you for those who cannot believe: your love is always offered.

Risen Christ, you are the support of those who encounter difficulties and discouragement: lead us on the path of eternity.

Risen Christ, we pray to you for those who have been victims of violence and humiliation: come to heal their wounds.

Risen Christ, you guide us by your Spirit: gather all the nations into your Kingdom.

OUR FATHER

PRAYER

Jesus our joy, by your continual presence within us, you lead us to give our life. Even if we forget you your love remains, and you send your Holy Spirit upon us.

or

Bless us, Christ Jesus; you show us where to find rest for our hearts.

SONGS

Time of the Church   13

PSALM

My soul, give praise to the Lord;
I will praise the Lord all my days,
make music to my God while I live.

They are happy who are helped by Jacob's God,
whose hope is in the Lord their God,
who alone made heaven and earth,
the seas and all they contain.

It is the Lord who keeps faith for ever,
who is just to those who are oppressed.
It is God who gives bread to the hungry,
the Lord, who sets prisoners free.

The Lord who gives sight to the blind,
who raises up those who are bowed down,
the Lord, who protects the stranger
and upholds the widow and the orphan.

It is the Lord who loves the just
but thwarts the path of the wicked.
The Lord will reign for ever,
Zion's God, from age to age.

from Psalm 146

READING

Paul wrote: For this reason I bow my knees before the Father, from whom every family in heaven and on earth takes its name. **I pray that,** according to the riches of his glory, he may grant that you may be strengthened in your inner being with power through his Spirit, and that **Christ may dwell in your hearts through faith, as you are being rooted and grounded in love.** I pray that you may have the power to comprehend, with all the saints, what is the breadth and length and height and depth, and to know the love of Christ that surpasses knowledge, so that you may be filled with all the fullness of God.

Ephesians 3,14-19

or

Many of Jesus' disciples turned back and no longer went about with him. So Jesus asked the twelve, "Do you also wish to go away?" Simon Peter answered him, "Lord, to whom can we go? You have the words of eternal life. We have come to believe and know that you are the Holy One of God."

John 6,66-69

SONG

SILENCE

INTERCESSIONS

God our Father, you gather us into the communion of your Church: give us life by your love.

God our Father, you never take back your call and your gifts: give us life by your love.

Son of the living God, your faithfulness enables us to remain always faithful to you: give us life by your love.

Son of the living God, you are familiar with our trials and our poverty: give us life by your love.

Holy Spirit, in our lives you stimulate a desire for peace and justice: give us life by your love.

Holy Spirit, your road leads us towards all who suffer in our society: give them life by your love.

Holy Spirit, you have placed gifts in our hearts to make us creators of communion: give us life by your love.

OUR FATHER

PRAYER

Christ Jesus, enable us to forge a steadfast heart to remain faithful to you. Risen Lord, you send upon us the light of your forgiveness. That is the perfect gift. And for each person, to dare to forgive awakens God's joy in us.

or

Jesus our peace, obtain for us the greatest of joys: to have one mind, one love, one soul.

SONGS

Time of the Church   14

SONG

PSALM

Praise God in his holy place,
sing praise in the mighty heavens.
Sing praise for God's powerful deeds,
praise God's surpassing greatness.

Sing praise with sound of trumpet,
sing praise with lute and harp.
Sing praise with timbrel and dance,
sing praise with strings and pipes.

Sing praise with resounding cymbals,
sing praise with clashing of cymbals.
Let everything that lives and that breathes
give praise to the Lord. Alleluia!

Psalm 150

READING

Therefore, since we are surrounded by so great a cloud of witnesses, let us also lay aside every weight and the sin that clings
so closely, and let us run with perseverance the race that is set
before us, looking to Jesus the pioneer and perfecter of our
faith, who for the sake of the joy that was set before him
endured the cross, disregarding its shame, and has taken his
seat at the right hand of the throne of God. Consider him who
endured such hostility against himself from sinners, so that you
may not grow weary or lose heart.

Hebrews 12,1-3

Jesus said: As the Father has loved me, so I have loved you; abide in my love. If you keep my commandments, you will abide in my love, just as I have kept my Father's commandments and abide in his love. I have said these things to you so that my joy may be in you, and that your joy may be complete. This is my commandment, that you love one another as I have loved you. No one has greater love than this, to lay down one's life for one's friends.

John 15,9-13

SONG

SILENCE

LITANY OF PRAISE

With the prophets and all who have prepared your coming, Lord, we bless you.
—Glory to you, O Lord.

With the Virgin Mary, our soul magnifies the Lord.
—Glory to you, O Lord.

With the apostles and evangelists, Lord, we give you thanks.
—Glory to you, O Lord.

With the martyrs of the faith, Lord, we consecrate our lives to you.
—Glory to you, O Lord.

With all the holy witnesses to the Gospel, Lord, we worship you.
—Glory to you, O Lord.

With your entire Church, spread across the world, Lord, we sing your praises.
—Glory to you, O Lord.

OUR FATHER

PRAYER

God of all eternity, Savior of every life, in the footsteps of the holy witnesses to Christ down through the ages, from the apostles and the Virgin Mary to those of today, enable us to dispose ourselves inwardly day by day to place our trust in the Mystery of the Faith.

or

Living God, we praise you for the multitudes of women, men, young people and children who, across the earth, are striving to be witnesses to peace, to trust and to reconciliation.

SONGS

INDEX OF PSALMS

INDEX OF BIBLE READINGS

Other Taizé selections available from GIA Publications, Inc.

Recordings

Sing to God	CD-380	CS-380
Veni Sancte Spiritus	CD-325	CS-325
Jubilate	CD-284	CS-284
Songs and Prayers from Taizé	CD-266	CS-266
Canons and Litanies		CS-203
Cantos de Taizé		CS-201
Alleluia	CD-194	CS-194
Wait for the Lord	CD-173	CS-173
Resurrexit		CS-169
Taizé in Rome		CS-157
Taizé: Cantate		CS-156

Videos

Praying with the Songs of Taizé	VHS-391
Pilgrims and Friends	VHS-197
Taizé: That Little Springtime	VHS-196

Books

A Meaning to Life	G-4755
Peace of Heart in All Things	G-4649

Music Editions

Songs and Prayers from Taizé	G-3719
Cantos de Taizé	G-2974
Music from Taizé, Volume 2	G-2778
Music from Taizé, Volume 1	G-2433

The Letter from Taizé

Subscriptions: Letter from Taizé, 71250 The Taizé Community, France.

Other Taizé selections available from Cassell plc

Books

Songs and Prayers from Taizé	0-264-67256-9
The Story of Taizé	0-264-67170-8
His Love is a Fire	0 264-67210-0
No Greater Love	0-264-67253-4

Recordings

Songs and Prayers from Taizé (CD)	0-264-67299-2
Songs and Prayers from Taizé (Cassette)	0-264-67273-9

Video

Praying with the Songs of Taizé	0-264-67458-8